SECRET
ROME

ROME

01 M

TO MY FRIENDS

PEGG MELFA...

THANK YOU
FOR *INSPIRING* ME

THIS BOOK WILL MOTIVATE YOU
TO COME AND VISIT AGAIN:
THE REAL SECRET OF ROME IS
SOME KIND OF ENERGY
YOU WILL BE NOW ABLE TO
BREATH !!!)

Jonglez

D0095872

Ginevra Lovatelli is the author of the first version of this guide. She organises original private tours to discover Rome.
Website: www.secretrome.com

Adriano Morabito, born and raised in Rome, still passionate about his city and its less well-known sites, has since 1999 focused his attention on urban speleology. He is one of the founders of "Roma Sotterranea", an association active in the exploration and study of underground tombs of historical and archaeological interest:
www.romasotterranea.it

Other contributors: **Jacopo Barbarigo, Marylène Malbert, Hélène Vuillermet** and **Viviana Cortes**

Alessandra Zucconi took most of the photos in this guide.
Find her work at www.goldenratio.biz

We have taken great pleasure in drawing up
Secret Rome and hope that through its guidance
you will, like us, continue to discover unusual,
hidden or little-known aspects of the city.
Descriptions of certain places are accompanied
by thematic sections highlighting historical details
or anecdotes as an aid to understanding the city in
all its complexity.
Secret Rome also draws attention to the multitude
of details found in places that we may pass every
day without noticing. These are an invitation to
look more closely at the urban landscape and,
more generally, a means of seeing our own city
with the curiosity and attention that we often
display while travelling elsewhere …

Comments on this guidebook and its contents,
as well as information on places we may not have
mentioned, are more than welcome and will enrich
future editions.
Don't hesitate to contact us:
• Éditions Jonglez, 17, boulevard du Roi,
  78000 Versailles, France
• E-mail: info@jonglezpublishing.com

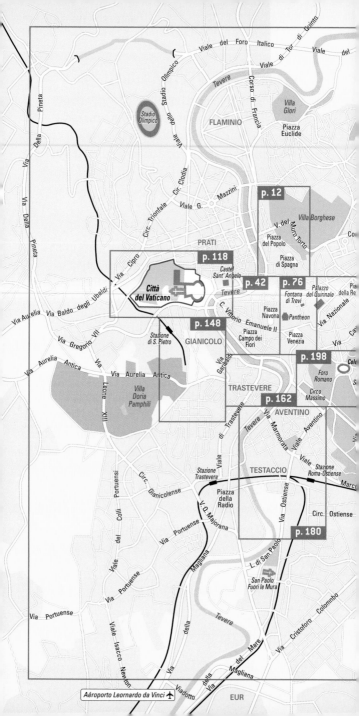

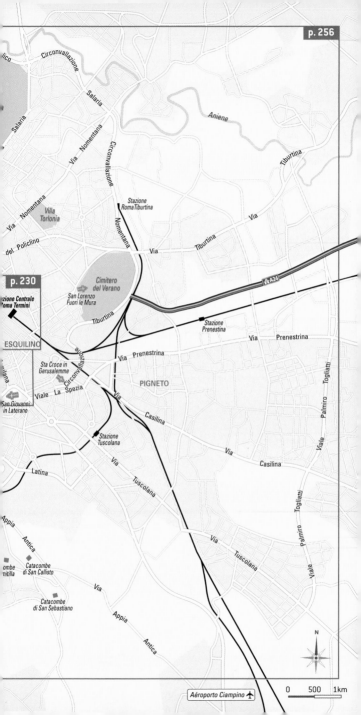

p. 256

p. 230

Circonvallazione

Salaria

Salaria

Via Nomentana

Aniene

Circonvallazione

Via Nomentana

Tiburtina

Via Nomentana

Villa Torlonia

Stazione Roma Tiburtina

Nomentana

del Policlino

Via

Via

Via

Tiburtina

Cimitero del Verano

zione Centrale oma Termini

San Lorenzo Fuori le Mura

ESQUILINO

Tiburtina

Stazione Prenestina

Via Prenestina

A24

Sta Croce in Gerusalemme

Via Prenestina

Via Prenestina

San Giovanni in Laterano

Viale La Spezia

Circonvallazione

PIGNETO

Togliatti

Via

Via Casilina

Palmiro

Stazione Tuscolana

Via

Casilina

Via

Casilina

Latina

Via Tuscolana

Togliatti

Appia Antica

Via

Palmiro

ombe itilia

Catacombe di San Callisto

Via Tuscolana

Viale

Catacombe di San Sebastiano

Via

Appia Antica

N

Aéroport Ciampino ✈

0   500   1km

CONTENTS

CENTRE WEST

CONTENTS

TRASTEVERE

AVENTINO - TESTACCIO

LATERAN - COLOSSEUM - FORO - CELIO

CONTENTS

OUTSIDE THE CENTRE

INDEX

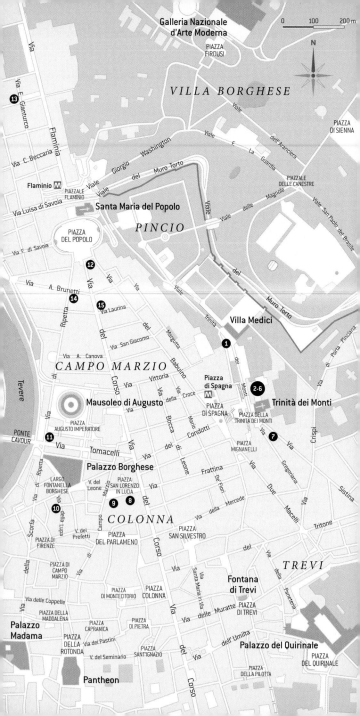

CENTRE NORTH

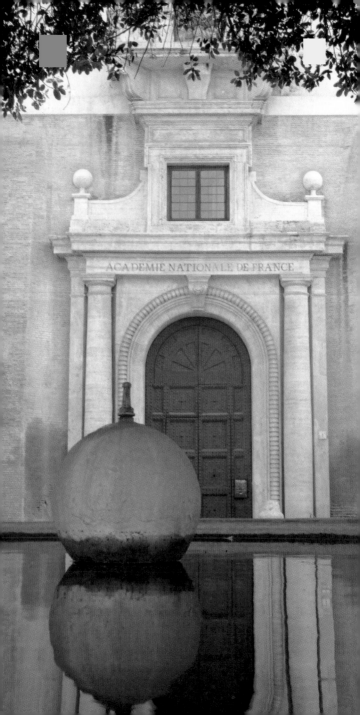

THE CANNON BALL OF VIALE DELLA TRINITÀ DEI MONTI FOUNTAIN

❶

Viale Trinità dei Monti, opposite Villa Medici
Metro: A - Spagna

A real cannon ball in the centre of a fountain

I n line with the entrance to the Villa Medici is a majestic granite fountain that, with the panorama of Rome in the background, has inspired many artists, such as the painter Jean-Baptiste Camille Corot who immortalised the scene in 1826.

The basin of the fountain came from San Salvatore in Lauro; Cardinal Ferdinando de' Medici is thought to have acquired it from the monastery in 1587 for 200 ecus. The setting, however, came from a square close to San Pietro in Vincoli. It was probably constructed around 1589 by Annibale Lippi, one of the architects of the Villa Medici.

There is an incredible story about the provenance of the cannon ball from which the water flows in the centre of the fountain.

In 1655, Queen Christina of Sweden, a prominent figure in 17th-century Roman life, is said to have had the cannon fired from Castel Sant'Angelo in the direction of the Villa Medici in an attempt to wake up the master of the house to go hunting. Three traces of the impact on the heavy door of the Villa bear out this version of events, while one of the balls was recovered to be set into the fountain opposite …

At the time, however, the villa was no longer much used by its then owner, Cardinal Carlo de' Medici.

Another theory goes that Queen Christina (a bit of a loose cannon herself) had promised the painter Charles Errard, director of the Académie de France in Rome, to knock at his door at a certain time of day. At the appointed hour, she was still at Castel Sant'Angelo and found a way of keeping her word by having the cannon pointed at the door of Villa Medici … Note that this version is most certainly false: the Académie de France was established in 1666 with its headquarters at Sant'Onofrio (it only moved to the Villa Medici in 1803, having successively occupied several Roman palaces). What does seem sure, however, is that these legends grew up not only to justify the marks on the door, but also the impetuous character of Queen Christina of Sweden!

TRACES OF THE ACQUA VERGINE IN THE TOPOGRAPHY AND TOPONYMY OF THE TRINITÀ DEI MONTI DISTRICT

In 19 BC, Agrippa opened the aqueduct intended to supply the thermal baths that he had built on the Campus Martius, to the north of Largo Argentina. The source of the "virgin water" (Aqua Virgo, renamed Acqua Vergine when it was restored during the Renaissance) lay to the north-east of Rome at Salone, and reached the city after running mainly underground for 19 km. Its course can be traced on the surface, marked by various points of access to the water. For example, the aqueduct crosses the park of the Villa Medici diagonally north to south, where a well – a small white building at the edge of the villa's gardens – gives access to the water.

Another view of the aqueduct lies behind the grey door of No. 2B of Viale Trinità dei Monti, to the right of the Villa Medici. A plaque still reads, "Acqua vergine. Alla chiocciola del Pincio", indicating what the door conceals: a spiral staircase (*chiocciola*) that leads down some thirty metres to the ancient underground channel.

This water follows its underground course to feed the San Sebastianello reservoir, at the foot of the hill of that name. The modern reservoir (a plaque dates it to 1891) was built to replace a 16th-century cistern which stood at the bottom of the ramp that now leads up to Trinità dei Monti church, confirmed by the name of the street served by the metro, *Vicolo del Bottino* (Alley of the Reservoir). Inside this small building is another spiral staircase that leads to the upper vault of the aqueduct tunnel. This reservoir supplies many of the fountains in the district, such as those of the Villa Medici and the Fontano della Barcaccia in Piazza di Spagna, and of course the water spout in San Sebastianello's niche.

Sixteenth-century maps show that a church once stood on the site of this niche, so it may originally have been an apse set into the retaining wall of the church grounds and closing off the view from Via della Croce. Documents from the 17th century do indeed show a "San Bastiano chapel", which was dismantled during the construction of the Spanish Steps in the 18th century. A painting or shrine to Saint Sebastian once contained in the niche must surely have disappeared during redevelopment of the area. The apse-like shape and the name of the street are now the only signs of how things used to be. San Sebastianello's niche is now home to a more modest fountain over a Christian sarcophagus of the early 4th century depicting the deceased with the Good Shepherd. The resulting simple composition in a monumental space stands out against the spectacular backdrop of the Barcaccia Fountain (1629) in Piazza di Spagna, not to mention the Baroque display of the Trevi Fountain, completed in 1762; both fountains are also fed by the aqueduct.

TRINITÀ DEI MONTI CONVENT

Monastic Fraternities of Jerusalem
3 Piazza Trinità dei Monti
00187 Rome
• Open twice a week, Tuesday at 11am and Sunday at 09.15am, book
through (visitesguidees.tdm@libero.it)
• E-mail: maison.accueil.tdm@libero.it

*The
forgotten
convent*

Visitors to Trinità dei Monti church, with its rich fresco decoration by Daniele da Volterra, should not miss the convent of the same name that holds treasures whose value remains largely unrecognised. The entrance to the convent is at the top of the stairway to the left of the church.

The tour, led by a nun from the French religious order of the Monastic Fraternities of Jerusalem (to which the church was entrusted in 2006, replacing the Society of the Sacred Heart), takes in the convent cloister with its series of decorations and a small 19th-century chapel dedicated to the founding mother of the convent, before revealing the high points of the visit: two anamorphic paintings, an astrological ceiling and a refectory completely covered in trompe-l'œil frescoes (see following pages for details of these works). Depending on events in the convent, the guide sometimes finishes the tour with the "parrot" room and a corridor within the chapels from which Daniele da Volterra's extraordinary *Descent from the Cross* can be better appreciated.

The tour starts from the convent cloister decorated with a series of episodes from the life of Saint Francis of Paula (1416-1507), founder of the Order of Minims for whom this convent was initially established. Not all of these frescoes are of interest and some of them have been seriously damaged by later overlays and unfortunate restoration projects. Worth noting, however, is the work by the Cavalier d'Arpino, painter of the *Canonisation of Saint Francis of Paula* (first fresco on the right after the entrance to the cloister), as well as that of lesser-known artists such as Girolamo Massei, Cristoforo Roncalli, Paris Noforo Roncalli, or Giacomo Semenza. Between the windows is a series of portraits unusual to find in Rome: the kings of France, from Pharamond to Louis XIV, painted by Avanzino Nucci in 1616, before other artists continued this portrait gallery.

On the upper floor is a chapel recalling an Anglo-Saxon aesthetic unheard-of in the heart of Rome. A long, low room covered in woodwork and ex voto offerings holds a fresco (the source of a number of miracles) executed in 1844 by a novice known by the name of "Madonna of the Lily", or "Mater Admirabilis", ever since Pope Pius XI declared her as such during his visit of 1846.

THE PARROT ROOM

3

Trinità dei Monti convent
• Monastic Fraternities of Jerusalem - 3 Piazza Trinità dei Monti
00187 Rome • Open twice a week, Tuesday and Saturday mornings at
11am, book through Sister Silvia: 06 67 97 436 (phone Monday to Friday
between 8am and 1pm)
• E-mail: maison.accueil.tdm@libero.it

The remarkable parrot room (or room of the ruins) was painted by Charles-Louis Clérisseau (1721-1820), a student at the Académie de France in Rome from 1749 to 1754.

This work was commissioned by Father Lesueur to decorate his cell, where he presumably wished to be able to retreat as a hermit among the ancient ruins.

The room, including the vault, is entirely covered in frescoes showing a ruined Roman temple with vegetation growing through the walls open to the sky, sections of broken walls, crumbling beams and a few columns still standing. Clérisseau pushed reality to the limits in his depiction of the weeds and ivy growing in the cracks of the stonework, representing the chimney as a heap of ancient ruins and reproducing the brick structure of the building.

This room embodies the taste for antiquity, which was then in fashion, through the declination of a precise architectural vocabulary: Corinthian pillars and columns, imposing architrave, vault with octagonal box sections and central cornice, now open to the sky and boarded up with a random collection of planks. A parrot on an overhead beam looking down at the room has given its name to this painting, which has been praised by the German art historian Winckelmann.

WEDDING AT CANAAN *TROMPE-L'ŒIL*

Refectory of Trinità dei Monti convent
Monastic Fraternities of Jerusalem
3 Piazza Trinità dei Monti
00187 Rome
• Open twice a week, Tuesday at 11am and Sunday at 09.15am, book through (visitesguidees.tdm@libero.it)
• E-mail: maison.accueil.tdm@libero.it

> *An extraordinary trompe-l'œil completed in three days*

The former refectory of the Minims is home to a remarkable example of *trompe-l'œil* painting. This neutral room, devoid of any architectural ornament, is structured around the painting that runs from floor to ceiling.

The Jesuit Brother Andrea Pozzo (1642-1709) achieved the remarkable feat of a complete optical illusion by painting a life-size balustrade, a double row of *trompe-l'œil* columns that open up the perspective in the round towards the exterior, and a vaulted roof complete with painted box beams. As in the church of Sant'Ignazio, where Pozzo created incredible perspectives of the vault and cupola, you should stand on a particular spot – in the centre of the room in this case – to appreciate the perfection of the whole scene. You will find yourself at a banquet, an obvious theme considering the function of the room, representing the Wedding at Canaan. Seen from the entrance to the refectory are Jesus and Mary, rather than the bride and groom, as well as a jar-bearer who literally draws the observer into the picture. The effect is accentuated since the balustrade is absent, thus creating a direct link with the perpetrator of the miracle (turning water into wine). The married couple appear off to the side, and crowds of jostling people act as a foil to welcome the visitor to the celebrations. The wedding party musicians overlook the scene from a balcony above the entrance, over a portrait of Louis XIV. On the ceiling, the eye is drawn to the apotheoses of Saint Francis of Paula, founder of the Order of the Minims, and Saint Francis de Sales, also affiliated to this Order, as well as a representation of the Holy Trinity. Scenes from the life of Saint Francis of Paula are featured in the side niches above.

The story goes that Andrea Pozzo completed this work, which dates back to 1694, in the record time of three days and three nights. But no doubt he was helped by his assistants: it is fairly easy to spot the more clumsily executed figures that are not by the master, whose virtuosity is most evident in the delicately coloured draperies.

THE ANAMORPHIC FRESCOES OF TRINITÀ DEI MONTI CONVENT ❺

Trinità dei Monti convent
• Monastic Fraternities of Jerusalem
3 Piazza Trinità dei Monti - 00187 Rome
• Open twice a week, Tuesday at 11am and Sunday at 09.15am, book through (visitesguidees.tdm@libero.it)
• E-mail: maison.accueil.tdm@libero.it
• Note: the second anamorphic fresco is currently being restored

A quite astonishing optical illusion

On the upper floor of Trinità dei Monti convent, you can visit a corridor that runs right round the cloister and features two rare anamorphic paintings (see explanation opposite), the result of the residents' research on perspective. Until the 18th century, the convent housed French monks of the Order of Minims, some of whom were carrying out important scientific work, such as Father Emmanuel Maignan (1601-1676) and his disciple Father Jean-François Nicéron (1613-1646), both of whom held a special interest in optics and perspective. Their work in this field culminated in two anamorphic frescoes painted on the upper floor of the convent, on either side of the cloister, but there is some disagreement as to which monk they should be attributed.

Nicéron, who wrote a treaty on perspective, *Thaumaturgus opticus*, spent only ten months in Rome in 1642, but he probably assisted his master in executing one of the two frescoes, following the principles set out in his text.

The first anamorphosis, painted in grisaille, depicts Saint Francis of Paula at prayer, kneeling under a tree, an image that can be seen from the end of the corridor. But if you stand directly in front of the fresco, the figure of the saint disappears, recomposing as a marine landscape with a bay enclosed by hills. A port can be seen as well as towers, greenery and several figures. The scene is thought to be the region of Calabria in southern Italy where the saint lived, and shows episodes from his life. The two men in the water near a sailing boat, between two spits of land, recall the time when Saint Francis was refused passage by a boatman to cross the Strait of Messina, so he laid his cloak on the water and sailed across on it. Likewise, the figures lost in this desert landscape symbolise the hermit's way of life.

At the same level on the other side of the cloister is another anamorphic fresco, this time depicting Saint John the Baptist writing the Book of Revelation. A similar work can be found in Paris in the former convent of the Minims, which used to stand in what is now the Place des Vosges. The ideal vantage point to reveal the figure of the saint is on entering the room. But like the other painting, if you stand directly in front of the picture you see a landscape, that of the island of Patmos where Saint John received a vision of Christ.

WHAT IS ANAMORPHOSIS?

The basic principle of anamorphic perspective is to project the line of vision in order to present an image as it would appear to the observer at a given distance, and to transfer the drawing, or simply a grid, to the surface to be painted at an oblique angle.

The technique thus produces a deliberately distorted image that appears in its true shape if reflected in a certain kind of mirror (for curved anamorphoses for example) or viewed from a predetermined angle (most often oblique).

The most famous example of this technique is in Hans Holbein the Younger's painting *The Ambassadors* (1533), where the strange shape in the foreground is actually the distorted image of a human skull.

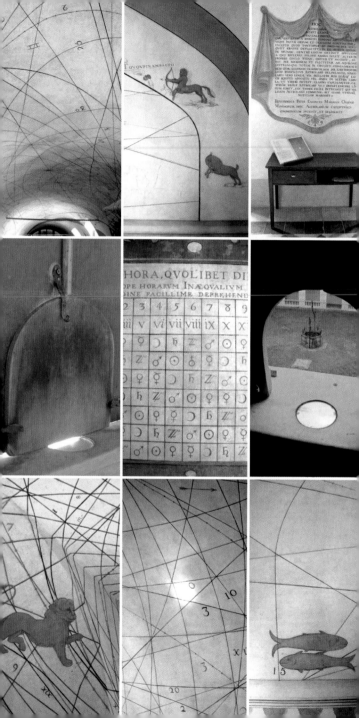

TRINITÀ DEI MONTI CONVENT SUNDIAL

Trinità dei Monti convent
• Monastic Fraternities of Jerusalem
3 Piazza Trinità dei Monti
00187 Rome
• Open twice a week, Tuesday at 11am and Sunday at 09.15am, book through (visitesguidees.tdm@libero.it)
• E-mail: maison.accueil.tdm@libero.it

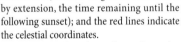

A rare catoptric sundial

The two anamorphic frescoes at the convent (see preceding double page) are separated by a sundial that fills the entire vault of the corridor overlooking the cloister. This ingenious system is the work of Father Emmanuel Maignan, for whom gnomonics (the art of building sundials) was but a secondary interest - mathematics, optics, and especially philosophy and theology, being the subjects that interested him most.

This example is a catoptric sundial, which shows the hours by the reflection of sunlight rather than by the shadow of a stylus. A mirror placed on the sill of the central window reflects a beam of light along the angle of 'incidence' to indicate the solar hour on the vault. A dish filled with water and mercury can similarly be used to achieve the same reflective effect.

The uniqueness of this astrolabe lies in the mass of information that can be derived from the vault according to the position of the beam of light. Arabic numerals in black, along the length of the black line, show the hour on the former Rome meridian (one hour in advance of the Greenwich meridian); using the Roman numerals (small and green, with green lines) Italian time can be read off (i.e. how long since sunset and, by extension, the time remaining until the following sunset); and the red lines indicate the celestial coordinates.

Also featured on the vault are the twelve signs of the zodiac and the names of cities of every continent, from the Solomon Islands to Babylon, from Mexico to the region of Goa; their local time is shown by the reflected sunlight.

Painted on the wall itself are several framed instructions on the usage and history of this sundial, while a painting identifies the planet corresponding to a given moment in time.

Another catoptric sundial, also built by Emmanuel Maignan, can be seen on the main floor of Palazzo Spada (see page 111).

THE FAÇADE OF PALAZZO ZUCCARI ❼

Via Gregoriana
• Metro: A - Spagna

> *Monsters on the façade*

Palazzo Zuccari occupies an area comprising the last part of Via Sistina and that of Via Gregoriana and its façade is probably the most curious and unusual in the city. The cornices of the main door and of the windows are all formed by gaping monsters' mouths.

Federico Zuccari, the famous Baroque artist, bought the land in 1590, struck by its wonderful location, and he built the house and the studio for himself and his children, drawing inspiration for the palace's façade from the "monstrous" style of the famous monsters of Bomarzo, close to Viterbo. This architectural whimsy was both criticised and admired, but in any case soon became the ideal house for artists in the area. Through the Accademia di San Luca, Zuccari left the dwelling to foreign artists, but his wishes were not respected and when the artist died, the building was passed on to another owner.

The Queen of Poland lived there from 1702 and for decades the house was the centre of high society in the city. After several changes of ownership, Zuccari's wish finally came true and the building became an inn for foreign artists. Winckelmann and Reynolds stayed there, David and Nazareni painted famous works there, and it appears in *Il Piacere* (The Child of Pleasure) by

Gabriele D'Annunzio. In 1900 Henrietta Hertz, the last owner, left her collection of paintings to the Italian state and the palazzo and its library to Germany, allowing for the creation of the famous Biblioteca Hertziana (Hertzian Library), specialised in art history and still open today to scholars with special letters of recommendation.

The building, which is closed to the public for restoration, is full of important works, such as the frescoes of Giulio Romano.

In the basement the ruins of the villa of Lucullo, from the end of the Roman Republic, were found.

POUSSIN'S TOMB ⑧

Church of San Lorenzo in Lucina
16a Via in Lucina
• Metro: A - Spagna
• Open Monday to Saturday 9am-12pm and 4:30pm-7:30pm,
Sunday 9:30am-1pm and 5pm-8pm
• Guided underground tour the first Saturday of the month at 5pm

> ❝ *Men of genius often herald their end with a masterpiece: it is their soul taking flight*

Poussin's tomb, commissioned by the French writer Chateaubriand between 1828 and 1832, when he was ambassador to Rome, is a white marble structure with a niche containing a bust of the painter. Below the bust figures a relief representation of his famous painting, *The Arcadian Shepherds*. Strangely sited between two of the church's side chapels (tombs are usually in the side chapels), the tomb was sculpted by Léon Vaudoyer, Paul Lemoyne and Louis Desprez, three pupils of the Villa Medici, the headquarters of the Académie de France since 1803.

Below the bas-relief, a Latin epitaph reads:

"Hold back your pious tears, in this tomb Poussin lives / He has given his life without himself knowing how to die / He is quiet here but if you want to hear him speak / It is surprising how he lives and speaks in his paintings."

Although much ink has been spilled over the phrase "Et in Arcadia ego" (see opposite), the existence of this tomb is probably only a straightforward homage to an artistic genius. As Chateaubriand said in *La vie de Rancé*, "Admirable tremor of time! Men of genius often herald their end with a masterpiece: it is their soul taking flight"

Guided underground tour: first Saturday of the month at 5pm.

ET IN ARCADIA EGO

The phrase "Et in Arcadia ego" was probably used for the first time in a painting by Guercino, *The Shepherds of Arcadia* (1618), commissioned by the Barberini family and now in the museum of the Galleria Nazionale d'Arte Antica of the Palazzo Corsini, opposite the Farnesina. The words are shown carved on a block of masonry, by way of comment on two shepherds leaning on their staffs contemplating a skull. The phrase next appeared in Poussin's first version (1628-1630) of a painting by the same name (now in the collection of the Duke of Devonshire at Chatsworth House in the UK), before gaining fame in the second version of the picture, probably painted around 1638 and now in the Louvre in Paris. Note that another, lesser-known painting kept at the Brive museum (France), entitled *Paysage aux bergers d'Arcadie* (anon., late 18th century), also bears the famous phrase and that a marble bas relief in the garden of the English property of Shugborough Hall also deals with the subject. The interpretation of these words carved in stone has been endlessly discussed. If Goethe, Schiller and Nietzsche understood it to mean, "I too have lived in Arcadia [and I have been happy there]", the most commonly accepted interpretation (due in part to art historian Erwin Panofsky) is "And even in Arcadia there I am [death]". In other words, even in an idyllic and paradisiacal place like Arcadia (see page 151), death is waiting for us all one day; stay humble and try to discriminate between the essential and the pointless and futile. Without going into all the more or less far-fetched interpretations, some have seen links between this phrase and the celebrated enigma of Rennes-le-Château, several aspects of which make reference to Poussin's paintings. In one of the coded manuscripts discovered at the site appear the names of Poussin and the Belgian painter Teniers; the inscription "Et in Arcadia ego" was also said to have been found there. Finally, some commentators have noted that the tomb in Poussin's painting and the surrounding countryside apparently corresponded to a tomb that once actually existed at Arques, near Rennes-le-Château. In 1978, researcher Franck Marie, like Pierre Jarnac in 1985, concluded that there was really nothing special about this tomb and that it had been dug in 1903 by the owner of the property, Jean Galibert, who had buried his mother and grandmother there. Their remains were exhumed and reburied elsewhere, most likely in the village cemetery, when the property was sold to Louis Lawrence, an American from Connecticut who had immigrated to the region. The latter, in turn, buried his mother and grandmother in the empty grave and had a tombstone bearing the inscription "*Et in Arcadia ego*" erected. Louis Lawrence's son, Adrien Bourrel, told Franck Marie and Pierre Jarnac that he had seen the tombstone erected in 1933, when he was a teenager. Nevertheless, a certain Pierre Plantard had the time to completely fabricate his "priory of Sion" while he was in prison and claimed that the tomb at Les Pontils had served as a model for Poussin's painting. This tomb was finally demolished in 1988 by the owner of the property, with the authorization of the local authorities, so as to stop the visitors who came from around the world in search of esoteric revelations, in vain. Thus, far from having any fabricated esoteric meaning, Poussin's painting and the phrase "*Et in Arcadia ego*" simply mean that death awaits us all one day.

THE RUINS OF AUGUSTUS' SUNDIAL

48 Via Campo Marzio
• Metro: A - Spagna
• Opening times: Visits on request by telephoning 06 336610144
or 06 33612607

The sundial obelisk

The spectacular Egyptian obelisk that is admired today in Piazza Montecitorio was once part of a giant sundial. The *Horologium Augusti* was in the centre of the gardens commissioned by the Emperor Augustus, which occupied all the Campo Marzio area at the time.

The clock was made up of a huge rectangular marble slab that measured 110 metres long and 60 metres wide according to some sources, and according to others it was even 150 metres by 70 metres. In the 9th century BC, the obelisk of the Pharaoh Psammetico II from the 6th century BC was brought to Rome by Augustus after the conquest of Egypt and was erected in the middle of the clock. It collapsed in the Middle Ages and remained buried for centuries. It was found in the middle of the 18th century and was erected in Piazza Montecitorio by Pope Pius VI, who tried to get the sundial working again. Bronze letters and rulers were set in the great marble face, and when the shadow of the obelisk would fall on it, it would indicate the time, the day and the month. The remains of the sundial, which had already been restored once before, towards the end of the 1st century AD, were discovered 5 metres underground about twenty years ago, in the basement of number 48, Via di Campo Marzio. Parts of the marble slab with the sundial line have been preserved, as have the transversal lines corresponding to two days, the inscriptions regarding the Leo, Taurus, Aries and Virgo signs of the Zodiac, and an indication of the winds that blew over the Aegean sea until the end of August.

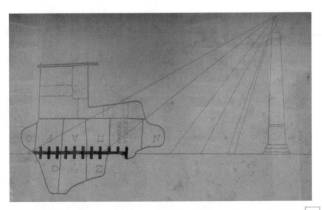

✝ BLA SIV.

BLESSING OF THE THROATS

Church of the Madonna del Divino Amore in Campo Marzio
12 Vicolo del Divino Amore
• 3 February, after mass
• Masses at 7:30am, 8am, 9am, 10am, 11am, 12pm and 6:30pm

> *Protect your throat from the rigours of winter!*

Once a year, in the deep midwinter, an extraordinary blessing helps you protect your throat and get through the winter safely. On 3 February, the feast day of Saint Blaise, masses are held throughout the day at the church of the Madonna del Divino Amore in Campo Marzio. After each mass, the priest gives the blessing by holding two candles in the form of a cross and touching people on the throat with them, repeating: "Through the intercession of Saint Blaise, bishop and martyr, may God deliver you from ailments of the throat and from every other evil, in the name of the Father, the Son and the Holy Ghost." The source of this tradition is the life of the saint himself (see below).

WHY IS SAINT BLAISE INVOKED TO PROTECT THE THROAT?

Born in the 3rd century AD in Armenia, Blaise was elected bishop of Sebaste. When the Christians began to be persecuted under Diocletian, he retreated to a cave surrounded by wild beasts, where he carried out several miracles including saving a child who was choking on a fishbone stuck in his throat. Blaise laid his hands on the child and prayed that he and all those who asked in his name should be healed, thus saving the child's life. Shortly afterwards, at his command, a wolf gave back a pig that it had seized from a poor woman. She later killed the pig and brought him its head and feet, with a candle and some bread. He ate the meat and

told her that whoever lit a candle in a church dedicated to him would reap the benefit. These two incidents were the source of the tradition of blessing the throat with wax candles.

Tortured with an iron comb or rake, Blaise was finally beheaded in 287 or 316, according to different sources.

INNUMERABLE RELICS OF SAINT BLAISE

Blaise is probably the Roman Catholic saint with the greatest number of "official" relics. If all those who claim possession are to be believed, Saint Blaise would have had over a hundred arms. Although his body is said to be buried at Maratea, in southern Italy, another body lies at San Marcello in Rome. The church of Santi Biagio e Carlo ai Catinari (Biagio is Italian for Blaise) allegedly retains the saint's "throat bone".

Traditional saying: "If on Candlemas day it be shower and rain, winter's gone and will not come again."

THE CASK OF THE BOTTICELLA FOUNTAIN

Via di Ripetta
• Between the churches of San Girolamo degli Schiavoni and San Rocco

The remarkable fountain known as the Botticella (little barrel), between Via di Ripetta and Piazza Augusto Imperatore, was erected in 1774 by the guild of innkeepers and boatmen of the former port of Ripetta, where ships loaded with merchandise used to dock.

Opposite San Rocco, the innkeepers wanted to build a fountain representing a porter to commemorate all those who unloaded the

> *Near the church of San Rocco (Saint Roch), patron saint of innkeepers, is a fountain dedicated to wine porters ...*

wood, wine, vegetables, and other goods arriving in Rome by river. Yet the figure of the wine porter was not chosen at random; among all the goods arriving in the port of Ripetta, the most coveted was wine. All the casks sent from the north of ancient Latium were first traded here. The porters spent their time wine-tasting in front of the church of Saint Roch, patron of innkeepers, in a jovial atmosphere.

The present site of the fountain, between the churches of San Girolamo degli Schiavoni and San Rocco, in a niche of the archway that links them, dates back to the 1940 renovation of the zone around the Mausoleum of Augustus. Several sources record that this fountain was formerly set against the façade of a neighbouring building, now demolished.

The figure of the porter is recognisable by his beret worn at an angle, typical headgear of that corporation. The fountain was paid for by Pope Clement XIV (1705-1774, elected pope in 1769), as recalled by the inscription with its distinctive lettering, the figures of which do not respect the tradition of Roman numerals. Clement XIV has been rendered as Clement XIIII, while the date, 1774, also has some inverted or unaligned figures - probably following the fashion of the day.

This fountain, like the Trevi, Barcaccia and so many others, is fed by the Acqua Vergine (Aqua Virgo), whose source is 12 km from Rome, and from which water is still brought into Rome today via Agrippa's aqueduct.

Rome possesses another fountain depicting a porter and barrel. Between Collegio Romano and Via del Corso, the *Facchino* (porter) fountain on Via Lata is dedicated to water carriers.

THE DINNER AT EMMAÜS IN SANTA MARIA DI MONTESANTO

Church of Santa Maria di Montesanto
198 Via del Babuino - Piazza del Popolo
• Mass of the Artists: Sundays at 12pm

"

An anachronistic painting

I n the chapel of Souls in Purgatory, to the right in the church of Santa Maria di Montesanto, is a recent painting so anachronistic as to be an unexpected find in a Roman church.

Painted by Riccardo Tommasi Ferroni (1934-2000), *The Dinner at Emmaüs* takes up the well-known theme of the Emmaus pilgrims. Although the composition of the painting is classical, there are several striking details, such as the very contemporary trainers worn by one of the pilgrims who is nonchalantly leaning on the table chatting with Jesus, who himself is wearing a traditional light-coloured robe.

THE ARTISTS' CHURCH
Santa Maria di Montesanto is the artists' church. From late October to 29 June, music is played during the Sunday midday mass. An actor generally reads the texts and, at the end of the mass, a prayer for the artists is said.

The Mass of the Artists tradition began on 7 April 1951, ten years after a group of artists had begun to hold meetings with Monsignor Ennio Francia, to celebrate a mass in their honour.

THE TRIDENT: THREE ROUTES FOR PILGRIMS TO ROME
Diverging from Piazza del Popolo, the three streets known as the Trident were planned in the 17th century to direct pilgrims towards their itineraries when entering the city by the north gate. By taking the former Via Leonina (now Via Ripetta, built by Pope Leo X in 1515) they rejoined the Tiber and the Sant'Angelo bridge and then went on to Saint Peter's.

The former Via Clemenza (now Via del Babuino, opened in 1525 by Clement VII) headed in the direction of Piazza di Spagna and then on to Santa Maria Maggiore. Finally, the former Via Lata (now Via del Corso) led to San Giovanni in Laterano.

THE FIRST KNOWN GROTESQUES OF THE RENAISSANCE
The church of Santa Maria del Popolo is home to a superb painting by Pinturicchio, in the first chapel to the right of the main entrance. The painted decorations to each side of it are the first representation of grotesques following the discovery of the Domus Aurea (see page 219).

HENDRIK CHRISTIAN ANDERSEN MUSEUM

Villa Helene, 20 Via Pasquale Stanislao Mancini
- Tel: 06 3219089, 06 3234000, 06 3241000
- Fax: 06 3221579
- Tram: 2, 19
- Metro: A - Flaminio
- Open Tuesday to Sunday, 9am-8pm
- Opening times for the museum's cafe on the first floor: 10:30am-6pm
- Admission free

> **The artist's residence as a museum**

Villa Helene is an elegant building just a stone's throw from the Tiber. It was built in 1922 by the Norwegian sculptor and painter Hendrik Christian Andersen, who moved to Rome in 1897. The villa is an extremely interesting example of a studio-residence transformed into a museum, and it was reopened to the public after restoration work in 1999. The ground floor is composed of the studio, where Andersen planned and created his works, which he then exhibited to the public in the other room, the gallery. There are about forty large plaster and bronze sculptures exhibited in both areas. The first floor, once the artist's residence, has drawings, paintings and smaller sculptures.

Over two hundred sculptures, as many paintings and about three hundred pieces of graphic art including drawings and plans make up a collection that is not only surprising in terms of its size, but also and especially because everything, except the paintings, is dedicated to the artist's sole great plan, the creation of a "world city". To disseminate his idea of a utopian modern city that would be an experimental centre of new ideas for art, philosophy, religion and science, Andersen and the architect Ernest Hebrard published an illustrated book in 1913 entitled *Creation of a World Center of Communication*.

A visit in spring is particularly pleasant as you can sit and have something to drink in the Caffè del Museo and take a break in the sun on the lovely first-floor terrace.

SQUATRITI ⓮

29 Via di Ripetta
• Tel: 06 3610232
• Metro: A - Spagna or Flaminio
• Open Tuesday afternoon to Saturday morning, 9am-1pm
and 3:30pm-7:30pm

Dolls' hospital

In Via di Ripetta, the artistic restorers' shop, Squatriti is situated at the corner of Via del Vantaggio.

The grandmother of Federico, the young man who still works here today, opened this strange workshop in 1953, where initially only vases from archaeological excavations and painted Italian ceramics were restored until Federico's father branched into new activities with his wife, who began restoring fans and dolls. Today it is mostly because of the dolls that this place attracts the attention of passers-by.

The shop is tiny and you instantly have the feeling of entering a timeless place. Federico and his mother work intently at two small counters around which there is hardly any room to walk. Objects fill the shelves, most of the floor and even the ceiling: vases, Italian ceramics, items made from ivory, wax, papier-mâché, plaster, porcelain and marble, but above all lots of dolls piled up in the shop windows, giving this workshop the atmosphere of an old horror movie.

From the 1960s onwards, only porcelain or cellulose dolls were repaired, and once industrial plastic dolls were introduced these earlier dolls became collectors' items.

Even if you have nothing to be repaired, it is nevertheless worth your while glancing around the shop and meeting the owners.

GOETHE HOUSE

18 Via del Corso
• Tel: 06 32650412
• www.casadigoethe.it
• Metro: A - Spagna or Flaminio
• Open Tuesday to Sunday, 10am-6pm

A stage in the "Journey to Italy"

Turning into Via del Corso from Piazza del Popolo, a few metres ahead of you is the house in which Johann Heinrich Wilhelm Tischbein welcomed his friend and great poet Johann Wolfgang von Goethe from 1786 to 1788.

In the numerous rooms of this large townhouse, there is a large collection of letters, books, notes and copies of drawings regarding the poet's journey to Italy and works by Tischbein himself who painted, among other things, Goethe in daily life during his Roman sojourn.

Thanks to these testimonies it is interesting to learn what it really meant to travel in Italy at the end of the 18th century. Apart from the permanent exhibition, interesting temporary exhibits are also set up with debates and book presentations.

CENTRE SOUTH

MASS IN ARAMAIC CHURCH OF SANTA MARIA ❶ IN CAMPO MARZIO

45/A Via di Campo Marzio
• Metro: A – Spagna or Barberini
• Mass in Aramaic: Sundays at 10:30am

> *Mass in the language of Jesus*

Hidden away in one of the most frequented parts of the historic centre, Santa Maria in Campo Marzio is an Eastern Catholic church of the Syrian-Antiochene rite but obedient to Rome, in which mass is celebrated in Aramaic at 10:30 every Sunday morning. The often sparse congregation and the blend of three languages in which the mass is said (Aramaic, Arabic and Italian), together with the majestic architecture of the church, creates an ambience especially propitious to contemplation. After the service, worshippers are commonly invited to take coffee with the Patriarch.

The church dates back to the 8th century, when nuns fleeing from Constantinople during the persecution arrived in Rome and founded a convent. It was then acquired by the Benedictine nuns and enlarged to the size it is today, becoming one of the most important convents in the city.

The entrance from the street leads to a splendid courtyard with a distinctive tau cross shape, an oasis of peace within the bustling city centre. It was designed by De Rossi, who was also responsible for reconstructing the church at the end

of the 17th century. At the end of the courtyard, a very beautiful cloister with a central fountain can be glimpsed through a glass door, as well as one side of the church of San Gregorio Nazianzeno with its delicate little Romanesque belfry. This part of the complex is not open to visitors as it is managed by the Italian Chamber of Deputies, which has undertaken major restoration work. The convent had fallen into serious disrepair and was expropriated after 1870, since when it has been occupied by various public offices.

THE CHURCH OF SANT'IGNAZIO ❷

Piazza di Sant'Ignazio
- Metro: A – Spagna or Barberini
- Bus: 116, 116T
- Opening times: Monday to Sunday 7:30am-12:30pm and 3pm-7:30pm

A flat dome

Founded by Cardinal Ludovisi in 1626 and built in several phases until 1662, the church of Sant'Ignazio has a peculiar aspect that goes unnoticed by almost all visitors: the cupola, which at first glance is nothing special as regards its decoration and dimensions, was in fact never built because of technical problems. The circular space for the dome, which is in fact flat, was painted using the *trompe l'oeil* technique by Father Andrea Pozzo. This work, known as the *Gloria di Sant'Ignazio* (Glory of Saint Ignatius) was painted in the vault of the nave with impressive perspective. The sensation felt once inside the church is strange, walking from the centre of the nave in the direction of the altar while looking at the skylight of the cupola. Little by little as you approach, the initial perspective no longer works and you realise that there is, in fact, no cupola.

❸

THE MONUMENTAL HALL OF COLLEGIO ROMANO

27 Via del Collegio Romano
- Open Tuesdays, Wednesdays and Thursdays 9:30am-1:30pm
- Tel.: 06 6797877

Lovers of art or archaeology, ancient books and great Baroque library enthusiasts, will take great pleasure in exploring the spectacular Sala Crociera (cruciform hall) of Collegio Romano, or even in studying in the sumptuous reading room attached to it.

The immense hall in the form of a cross, as its name indicates, is disconcertingly beautiful. The walls that form the arms of the cross are entirely covered in books, most of them ancient and rare. The superb shelving where they are stacked was built especially for the library in the 17th century, at the time when the hall was the main library of the college founded by Saint Ignatius of Loyola and modelled on the University of Paris.

More recently, this hall and the adjoining reading room were part of the National Library of Rome, until the latter moved into its present site at Castro Pretorio.

Since 1989, these halls have been occupied by the Library of Archaeology and History of Art, and the collection includes a vast number of volumes donated by archaeologists, art and architecture historians, as well as a collection of art gallery catalogues, with sections devoted to theatre, music, heraldry and Oriental art, besides an exceptional collection of catalogues from the principal salerooms dating from the 19th century onwards.

BIBILIOTECA CASANATENSE

Via Sant'Ignazio, 52
• Closed Sundays, 2nd and 3rd weeks of August
• Free guided tours on request
• Tel.: 06 69760328 or 06 69760334
• promozione.casanatense@biblioroma.sbn.it

A sumptuous monumental hall

With the exception of employees and a few researchers, hardly anyone knows that the sumptuous Casanatense Library is open regularly to the public for regular exhibitions, conferences, performances and concerts, and can even be visited free of charge upon request.

This library was founded by the Dominican friars of the Monastery of Santa Maria sopra Minerva in Rome at the request of Cardinal Girolamo Casanate, and inaugurated in 1701 in a structure within the Minerva cloister specially designed by the architect A. M. Borioni.

To the 25,000 original volumes that the cardinal bequeathed to the library were added many others acquired by the Dominicans over the years. Through their contacts with the main European booksellers, they sought out both antique and modern volumes to build up a "universal library" of texts on theology, economics and Roman law, as well as other scientific and artistic works.

In 1884, the Dominican librarians were finally replaced by civil servants when the library was forfeited to the Italian state. Since then it has formed part of the Ministry of Culture with a collection of over 350,000 works.

The splendid salone (hall), measuring 60.15 by 15.30 metres, is home to some 55,000 illustrated works dating from the 16th to the 18th centuries, displayed on magnificent wooden shelves built by the sculptor Marchesi and the gilder Cantoni to a design by Borioni. The shelving, divided by a single gallery halfway up, covers the walls from floor to ceiling, bathed in a perfectly uniform flood of light from the windows pierced in the vaulting above.

The coat of arms of the Casanate family can be seen (a tower surmounted by an eight-pointed star), the same symbol found on the library decorations and stamped on each object in the collection. This includes two magnificent 18th-century globes (the Earth and the Heavens), drawn in pen and wash by Abbot Moroncelli, a celebrated cosmographer, geographer and topographer, as well as an ancient copper armillary sphere surmounting the statue of Cardinal Casanate, created in 1708 by the French sculptor Pierre Le Gros.

Note, to the right of the entrance, the series of *trompe-l'œil* works that forms part of a door, often left open, behind which is concealed a spiral staircase.

THE HIDDEN SYMBOLISM OF BERNINI'S ELEPHANT-OBELISK

Piazza della Minerva

⑤

> *A symbol of the resurrection of the body*

Although Bernini's curious elephant-obelisk is of course famous in Rome, its symbolism is much less well-known. Why did Bernini design such an unusual sculpture? What does it signify? Bernini's design for the base of the obelisk, a stone elephant, is very similar to an engraving that appeared in *Hypnerotomachia Poliphili* [Poliphilo's Dream of the Strife of Love], the extraordinary Renaissance *roman-à-clef* published in Venice in 1499 (portraying well-known real people disguised as fictional characters - see the following double-page spread). While for the Egyptians, the obelisk symbolised the "divine rays of the Sun", the great mass of the elephant symbolised the Earth. With its trunk, it draws up water (the rain) which flows through the interior; the Earth is nourished, and with the help of the Sun (the obelisk) which traverses the Earth (the elephant), the grain is fertilised, so that it can be reborn and flourish. In the text that inspired Bernini, the reader enters the elephant, inside of which a man and a woman are represented. The full force of the symbol is thus revealed: besides the grain which is reborn and fertilised, the elephant-obelisk symbolises the resurrection of the body, a belief transmitted by the Egyptians (notably in the Book of the Dead) to the Hebrews and Christians to become a central element of Christianity. At the Last Judgment (like the biblical Jonah who emerges from the

belly of the whale), man will leave the Earth to rise again from the dead. Pope Alexander VII, who commissioned the monument from Bernini in 1667, to be erected on the site of a former Temple of Isis, possessed a copy (annotated in his own hand) of *Hypnerotomachia Poliphili* and it was he who had the Latin phrase inscribed on the base recalling the immense wisdom passed down from ancient Egypt.* Remember that in Christian doctrine, the resurrection of Christ foreshadows that of all men and women at the Last Judgment. Finally, the Bernini sculpture also bears an eight-pointed star. The figure 8, for Christians, is the symbol of resurrection.

There is another elephant bearing an Egyptian obelisk at Catania, Sicily.

*Sapientis Ægypti / insculptas obelisco figuras / ab elephanto / belluarum fortissima / gestari quisquis hic vides / documentum intellige / robustae mentis esse / solidam sapientiam sustinere [These symbols of the science of Egypt, which you see engraved on the obelisk borne by the elephant, the most powerful of all animals, take them as the precept that a strong mind is needed to support a solid knowledge]

THE UNREQUITED LOVE OF LORENZO DE' MEDICI: AN INSPIRATION FOR POLIPHILO AND SHAKESPEARE?

The doomed love affair of Lorenzo de' Medici and Lucrezia Donati (who was married to Niccolo Ardinghelli against her will) seems to have directly inspired Poliphilo's quest: same name, same events, same timescale (1462-1464)...

The love life of Lorenzo the Magnificent is also thought to have provided the material for Francesco Cei, a poet close to Lorenzo, in his poem *Giulia e Romeo* which directly inspired Shakespeare to write the famous *Romeo and Juliet*.

POLIPHILO'S DREAM OF THE STRIFE OF LOVE, AN EXTRAORDINARY HUMANIST ROMANCE THAT DIRECTLY INSPIRED THE GARDENS OF VERSAILLES, BOBOLI (FLORENCE) AND BERNINI'S CELEBRATED ELEPHANT-OBELISK IN ROME

Printed by Aldus Manutius in Venice in 1499, *Hypnerotomachia Poliphili* [Poliphilo's Dream of the Strife of Love] is perhaps the most complex *roman-à-clef* ever published. Illustrated with around 170 exquisite woodcuts, it is also considered one of the finest examples of early printing.

The book, written in a mixture of Italian, Latin, Greek, Hebrew, Arabic, Spanish, Venetian and a few other dialects, was long considered anonymous. Recent research, however, chiefly led by Emanuela Kretzulesco,* has pointed to Francesco Colonna, as the decorative first letters of each of the thirty-eight chapters spell out the following phrase: *Poliam Frater Franciscus Columna peramavit* ("Brother Francesco Colonna dearly loved Polia"). A nephew of Cardinal Prospero Colonna, Francesco Colonna was part of the circle of Enlightenment figures that included Cardinal Bessarion, the future Pope Pius II and Nicholas V, known as the Renaissance Pope, opposed to the succeeding popes and in particular to Alexander VI Borgia. At a time when the Borgias, against the advice of Pius II and Nicholas V, were seeking to grant the pontiff temporal as well as spiritual power, and the papacy was embarking on a dark period of its history, *Poliphilo's Dream* was consequently rendered deliberately obscure in order to escape papal censure. More than a story of Poliphile's love for Lucrezia, the book is a spiritual quest of a philosopher passionately devoted to divine wisdom (Athena Polias). Developing humanist themes, he transmitted in a cryptic way the spiritual testament of a circle of theologians united around Nicholas V, who had undertaken comparative studies of religious traditions going back to ancient Greece and Egypt with great openness of mind, thus reviving the heritage of Pope Sylvester II (Gerbert of Aurillac). In concurrence with the Florentine Platonic Academy of the Medici and Marsilio Ficino, this group notably included the architect Leon Battista Alberti and Prospero Colonna, as well as being a great inspiration to Pico della Mirandola, Leonardo da Vinci, Nicolaus Copernicus, Giordano Bruno and Galileo.

Poliphilo's Dream reveals that the best way to know God is through Nature, divine creation. With the help of the codes held in the *Hyeroglyphica* of Horus Apollo (Horapollo), it also illuminates the spiritual road that leads there. In an absolutely extraordinary fashion for anyone interested in understanding the background against which *Poliphilo's Dream* evolved, it is clear that it also closely inspired the gardens of Versailles or Boboli in Florence, as well as Bernini's celebrated elephant-obelisk in Rome through the numerous symbols scattered along Poliphilo's route.

WHAT DOES *HYPNEROTOMACHIA* MEAN?

The etymology of the term *Hypnerotomachia* is based on the following Greek words: *hypnos* (sleep) *eros* (love), and *mache* (fight).

*Les Jardins du songe. Poliphile et la mystique de la Renaissance. Paris, Magma (only in French and Spanish).

THE STAG OF SANT'EUSTACHIO CHURCH ❻

Piazza Sant'Eustachio

> **A stag's head in place of Christ's cross**

A vigilant pedestrian looking upwards in Piazza Sant'Eustachio might notice a curious detail: instead of the traditional Christian cross that surmounts churches the world over, the church of Sant'Eustachio is crowned with a stag's head, with a cross on top of it.

This curiosity owes its existence to the life of St Eustace, who converted to Christianity when he encountered a stag with a crucifix between its antlers.

SAINT EUSTACE

Martyred in Rome around 130 AD, St Eustace was originally named Placidus. After his conversion he took the name Eustace (Latin Eustachius), which signifies "constancy". His feast day is 20 September, believed to be the day of his death.

On his way to hunt in the forest one day, Placidus, a well-respected Roman soldier, came across a herd of deer, one of which seemed larger and more splendid than the others. He approached the herd to kill the stag and noticed that he bore a crucifix in his antlers. A divine voice spoke to the soldier, saying that it had come to save him. In the face of this miracle, and because his wife had had a similar dream the night before, the whole family was baptized.

Returning the next morning to the scene of the miracle, Eustace once again had a vision of Christ, who informed the saint that he was going to be put to the test but that Christ would never forsake him.

A few days later, plague overwhelmed the region. St Eustace lost his troops and his home was raided. He and his family fled to Egypt. His wife was held for ransom by the owner of the boat making the crossing, but Eustace journeyed on with his two children who were soon taken by wild animals, one by a lion and the other by a wolf. After some years, the family was finally reunited. His wife had not after all been defiled by the boat's captain, and the children had been saved by villagers. After refusing to sacrifice to pagan gods, however, the family was put to death by the Emperor Hadrian.

The same miracle was later attributed to St Hubert, who became patron saint of hunters.

THE BEST CAFÉ IN ROME?

Established in 1938, Caffé Sant'Eustachio, just opposite the church, serves what is probably the best coffee in Rome. Note that the waiters deliberately hide themselves from the customers' view when preparing the coffee, jealously guarding the secrets of how it is made.

Piazza Sant'Eustachio, 82. Tel. (39) 06.68802048

THE HOLY FACE OF JESUS AT SANTO STEFANO DEL CACCO

Church of Santo Stefano del Cacco
26 Via Santo Stefano del Cacco
• Opening times: The first Tuesday of the month at 4:30pm for veneration of the Holy Face and on Sundays at 11:30am for mass
• Tel.: 338 3478858

> **A sacred image left on the moon in 1968**

On the first Tuesday of the month, at 4:30pm, a remarkable ceremony takes place in the first chapel of the left aisle of the church, during which the icon known as the Holy Face of Jesus is venerated.

Strictly speaking, this image was painted in 1945 by Gertrude Mariani (Sister Zeffirina of the Sacred Heart), based on a miraculous vision said to have been experienced by Sister Pierina De Micheli.

On 31 May 1938, in Milan, she had had a dazzling apparition of the Virgin Mary holding in her hand a medal on which the face of Christ was imprinted. The Virgin told the nun that this medal would allow whoever carried it and came each Tuesday to pray before the Holy Sacrament, to protect themselves against evil and enjoy the mercy of Jesus.

Jesus had already appeared to Sister Pierina De Micheli in 1932 and 1937, asking her to pray while contemplating his face.

The cult of the medal of the Holy Face was approved in August 1940 by the Archbishop of Milan and spread by, among others, Abbot Ildebrando Gregori, a Sylvestrine Benedictine monk who had been the spiritual father of Pierina De Micheli since 1940. In 1968, with the blessing of Pope Paul VI, a medal of the Holy Face was deposited on the moon by the American astronauts.

This beautiful church is commonly known as Santo Stefano del Cacco (Saint Stephen of the Monkey) because of an ancient Egyptian statue of the god Thoth represented with a dog's head, thought to be a monkey (*macacco*), which was found nearby (now exhibited in the Vatican Museums). The actual name of the church is Santo Stefano de Pinea: the marble pine-cone that can be seen on top of the belltower alludes to the name of the district.

The church, which probably dates back to the 9th century, has kept its basilica form with three naves divided by two rows of columns, and in the underground crypt there are still a number of very interesting tombstones. Pope Pius IV entrusted the church to the Sylvestrine monks in 1563. Its current appearance is the result of restoration work carried out in 1607.

SANCTUARY OF OUR LADY OF THE SMALL ARCH ⑧

Via di San Marcello
• Opening times: Monday to Saturday 6pm – 8pm for the recital of the rosary; Sunday 11am and 7pm for mass.

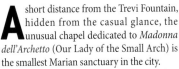

Virgin's eyes

A short distance from the Trevi Fountain, hidden from the casual glance, the unusual chapel dedicated to *Madonna dell'Archetto* (Our Lady of the Small Arch) is the smallest Marian sanctuary in the city.

The narrow street that joined Via di San Marcello to Via Dell'Archetto had a picture of the Virgin Mary painted on its wall. Domenico Muratori, a painter from Bologna and a student of Carracci, painted this picture for the marchioness Savorelli Papazzurri in 1690.

In 1696, the Virgin miraculously moved her eyes and the owner decided to display her within the street's arch for public veneration. In 1751, it was decided to close the entrances to the street with two gates, in order to protect the precious offerings that had accumulated. In 1796, the miracle, which was witnessed by several people, took place again and was recognised by

the Church. In the middle of the 19th century, the street was finally closed off completely and made into a chapel. The Savorelli Papazzurri family commissioned the architect Virginio Vespignani to build a small sanctuary, a jewel of neo-Renaissance art. It was solemnly inaugurated on 31 May 1851. The small temple, declared a national art monument and yet relatively unknown, contains sculptures by Luigi Simonetti and encaustic paintings by Costantino Brumidi, who, using the same technique, also painted the *Apotheosis of George Washington* fresco and became known as the "Michelangelo of the United States Capitol".

ORATORIO DEL SANTISSIMO CROCIFISSO

69 Piazza dell'Oratorio
- Tel/fax: 06 6797017
- Metro: A – Barberini or Spagna
- Opening times: 7am - 12pm and 4:30pm - 7pm

> *In memory of a miracle*

The Oratorio del Santissimo Crocifisso (Oratory of the Most Holy Crucifix), which is very beautiful but not well known, is in fact a large chapel that was built in memory of a miraculous event. On the night of 23 May 1519, the church of San Marcello al Corso was destroyed in a fire. At dawn, people ran to the site and discovered that the only thing that remained untouched in the smoking rubble was the wooden crucifix from the main altar.

In 1522 the crucifix put an end to a plague epidemic during a solemn procession organised to that effect and in 1526 the Confraternity of the Most Holy Crucifix was founded. In 1568 the oratory was built and became famous in the 17th century, as it was part of the creation of new forms of religious music. The interior is striking, and its walls are entirely frescoed by major artists of the time. Worth noting are Paris Nogari's *Procession of 1522*, Baldassarre Croce's *The Approval of the Statutes of the Confraternity*, Pomerancio's *The Miracle of the Crucifix*, Giovanni de' Vecchi's *The Exaltation of the Cross* and Niccolò Circignani's *The Miracle of the True Cross*.

The crucifix on the altar is an 18th-century copy of the miraculous one, which is now kept in the church of San Marcello. Since 1650, the 14th-century crucifix is carried in procession to St Peter's Basilica in holy years. Every year, on the day before Palm Sunday, the Archconfraternity, which heads some 120 confraternities scattered throughout various countries, organises a penitential procession along Via del Corso as far as San Marcello. The Archconfraternity also celebrates the miracle on 23 May and the Feast of the Exaltation of the Cross on 14 September with great solemnity.

KILL A MAN FOR A LIFELIKE MODEL!

A macabre legend has it that the sculptor of the crucifix murdered a man in his sleep to obtain the most realistic model he could find to represent the suffering of Christ on the Cross.

A UNIQUE VIEW OF THE TREVI FOUNTAIN

Palazzo Poli
53 Piazza dei Crociferi
• Metro: A – Barberini or Spagna
• Opening times: 9am - 7pm

Admire the Trevi Fountain without the tourists

Rome's National Graphics Institute, which is installed in both Palazzo Poli and Palazzo della Calcografia, was created in 1975 following the merger of the Calcografia Nazionale (National Centre for Prints) and the Gabinetto Nazionale delle Stampe (State Engraving Studio). It acquired the functions and the materials of the Calcografia Camerale (Vatican Printing Office) and has numerous printing presses, thousands of copper printing plates and sketches previously kept at Villa Farnesina.

The Palazzo della Calcografia was built in neo-classical style by Giuseppe Valadier to house the Reverend Apostolic Chamber's collection of copperplates. After recent restoration work, it now contains a printing museum and a new printing office; halls for temporary exhibits and archives of historic photos were added.

Visitors to an exhibition can admire the most famous water show in the city from a unique vantage point by just standing at the windows of the halls overlooking the fountain. They can thus enjoy the spectacle from far above the heads of the crowds.

The building, initially called Palazzo Ceri, changed its name in 1678 when it became the property of the Poli family who made some changes to it and enlarged it.

It would probably have remained just another ordinary building if Pope Clement XII had not organised a competition in 1731 to build a great fountain, choosing the beautiful façade of Palazzo Poli as its base.

In 1732 the building work began, based on Niccolò Salvi's designs.

Salvi's project, strongly influenced by Bernini, was such that the architectural part, the façade, the sculpture and the fountain all blended into one, thus giving birth to one of the most famous fountains in the world.

Pope Clement XII inaugurated the fountain in 1735. Pope Benedict XIV wanted a second ceremony in 1744, but the fountain remained unfinished even after Salvi's death in 1751 and was finally completed by Giuseppe Panini in 1762, under Pope Clement XIII.

PRINCESS ISABELLE'S APARTMENT

Colonna Gallery
66 Piazza Santi Apostoli
• Metro: A – Spagna or B – Colosseo
• Tel: 06 6784350 or 06 6794362
• Colonna Gallery is open on Saturday mornings from 9am - 1pm
• Admission: €7
• The apartments are open for private visits every day, all year round except August, for a minimum of ten people. Specialised guides available on request

A fantastic private visit

The gallery of Palazzo Colonna is certainly one of the most precious of Italy's artistic treasures and only insiders know that since 1946 it has been open to visitors once a week. Its extraordinary beauty can be enjoyed on Saturday mornings, by going through a small entrance hidden in the beautiful Via della Pilotta. Nor do many people know that while on private visits to the gallery, you can gain access to the rest of the palace. By contacting the palace administration and booking a private visit, it is possible to admire, alone and undisturbed, parts of the palace

that are closed to the public: the gallery, a series of adjacent rooms and the apartment of Princess Isabelle Sursock Colonna, who lived here until the end of the 1980s. This last visit is a unique experience: in the rooms of the apartment facing the interior garden some extraordinary art is to be found, such as the frescoes by the renowned painter Bernardino di Betto, known as Pinturicchio, refined works of Flemish masters, including engravings by Jan Bruegel the Elder, the rich collection of views by Gaspard Van Wittel, known in Italy as di Vanvitelli, and the decorations of Gaspard Dughet, Crescenzio Onofri, Cavalier Tempesta, Giacinto Gimignani and Carlo Cesi.

THE PALAZZO COLONNA CANNON BALL

Fired from the Janiculum Hill during a confrontation between French troops and Garibaldi's soldiers defending the Roman Republic in 1849, a cannon ball can amazingly still be seen on the grand staircase linking the two levels of the Palazzo Colonna gallery.

The projectile shattered one of the great windows and flew across the gallery before wedging itself in the steps, where the palace owners have left it as a reminder of the incident.

INTERNATIONAL CHRISTMAS CRIB MUSEUM ⑫

31/a Via Tor de' Conti
• Tel: 06 6796146
• Metro: B - Colosseo
• Opening times: from September to June, Wednesdays and Saturdays from 5pm-8pm; from 24 December to 6 January, Monday to Saturday 4pm-8pm, Sundays 10am-1pm and 4pm-8pm
• Admission free

A unique museum

A short distance from the Imperial Forums, the crypt of the church of Santi Quirico e Giulitta in via Tor de' Conti conceals a veritable wonder: the Museo Tipologico Internazionale del Presepio (International Christmas Crib Museum) and the headquarters of the Associazione Italiana Amici del Presepio (Italian Friends of the Crib Association). Founded in Rome in 1953, the association's goal is to gather together the numerous lovers of this tradition, to promote awareness of the crib from a religious, artistic, historic and technical point of view, and to organise courses and exhibitions all over Italy. Over three thousand pieces from the four corners of the globe are exhibited in the museum. The cribs range from sumptuous Neapolitan and Sicilian cribs to a tiny crib enclosed in a walnut shell, and they are made from various materials such as paper, ceramics, shells, cornhusks, plaster, cork and lead.

MONASTERIO DI SANTA FRANCESCA ROMANA DI TOR DE' SPECCHI

Via del Teatro di Marcello, 32
• Tel.: 06 6793565
• Open 9 March only, 8am-11:45am and 3pm-5pm
• Admission free

> *A convent open one day a year*

Located at the foot of the Capitoline Hill, the ancient residence where St Frances of Rome founded the religious congregation known as the Oblates is today still a convent that contains a number of treasures virtually unknown to the public. Once a year, however, an open day is held to let visitors discover the superb cloister and antique frescoes.

A stone doorway surmounted by a 17th-century fresco leads to a hall formerly used as stables. It is here that the Scala Santa (Holy Stairs) is found, leading to a small oratory dating from the 15th century, whose four walls are decorated with an astounding sequence of frescoes executed in 1468 and attributed to Benozzo Gozzoli (although some suggest they were painted by Antoniazzo Romano or a disciple of Piero della Francesca). Among the scenes illustrating the life of St Frances is the very beautiful panel showing the Virgin enthroned between St Frances, the angel and St Benedict, as well as a curious representation of Hell painted in a niche.

The visit continues into a great hall, which must have served as the refectory, where another cycle of monochrome frescoes covers an entire wall, as well as a small room in the medieval Tor de' Specchi [Tower of Mirrors], where Frances cloistered herself to pray and meditate and where her clothes and relics are preserved today in a coffer.

On Via del Teatro di Marcello, another entrance leads to the part of the convent dating from the 17th century. Having crossed the first two rooms with their fresco paintings where the "parlour" or reception room was situated, visitors enter a magnificent cloister, difficult to envisage from the outside, probably designed by the Baroque architect, Carlo Maderno. It is embellished with arcades on three sides, an octagonal well constructed in pale travertine stone, beautiful potted lemon trees, tombstones and archaeological artefacts embedded in the walls, recalling the life of the saint and the history of the convent. The buildings surrounding the cloister were erected in the early years of the 17th century to increase the number of cells, reflecting the growth of the congregation.

After the cloister, still on the ground floor, the tour continues with another room and a chapel, before mounting a flight of stairs to view another beautiful frescoed room and the choir of the Santissima Annunziata.

THE ABANDONED INFANTS BAS-RELIEF   🕐

22 Via delle Zoccolette

> ## *Abandoned girls destined to become prostitutes?*

A remarkable bas-relief set into the wall of 22 Via delle Zoccolette shows two swaddled infants. It commemorates an orphanage, now demolished, that used to take in abandoned children and give them an education.

The Palazzo dei "Cento Preti", built in 1576 by Domenico Fontana on the banks of the Tiber, was run by the congregation of that name as a hospice for beggars who had dedicated their life to Saint Francis. When the congregation moved elsewhere in 1715, the hospice became a church hospital, but the rear section giving onto Via delle Zoccolette was used as an orphanage. Among other domestic duties, girls learned embroidery, which could, if they had the opportunity, help them find a husband.

The name of the street also comes from the former orphanage, *zoccolette* meaning abandoned infants in the Roman dialect.

There are two versions of the source of this name. According to the first, the street is named after the little clogs (*zoccoli*) that the children wore,

whereas the second more common theory is that *zoccolette* used to designate prostitutes in Rome, as it does in the Neapolitan dialect. The term, through sympathy rather than malice, is thought to have been extended to the abandoned young girls who were condemned to end up walking the streets themselves, if they found neither work nor husband. Or the name could simply be due to the fact that some of the abandoned children were born to prostitutes.

For further information on abandoned children, see the article on the foundlings' wheel (page 129).

THE LEGEND OF PONTE FABRICIO'S FOUR HEADS
Ponte Fabricio

⓯

> *Boundary markers sacred to Hermes, or something more macabre?*

The heads that can be seen at either end of the parapet of Ponte Fabricio gave rise to the bridge's nickname, *Quattro Capi* ("four heads"). A strange legend is sometimes recounted to explain their presence.

During his pontificate (1585 to 1590), Sixtus V decided to have work done to restore the splendour of this ancient bridge, built in 62 BC. He called on four architects who could not agree on the best way to proceed. The pope, who had heard rumours of their discord, which was turning to hatred and sabotage, had them beheaded because of their non-Christian behaviour. The work had nevertheless been perfectly carried out, so the pope decided to erect a small monument in the men's honour and which would unite their four heads.

Although the legend is colourful, it seems that it is not entirely based on fact. These two pillars with two-faced Janus herms are thought to have once been boundary or crossroads markers depicting the head of Hermes, the god of roads and travellers. Hermes (sometimes identified with other gods or eminent personalities) was represented to mark boundaries and property limits.

THE HIDDEN TREASURES OF ROMAN BANKS

UniCredit Banca di Roma • Via del Corso 374
**Banca Finnat Euramerica, ABI (Associazione Bancaria Italiana) and Banco
Popolare: Palazzo Altieri** • Piazza del Gesù
BNL • Via Veneto 111 and 119
Banco di Sicilia. Palazzo Mancini • Via del Corso 270-272
Banca Antonveneta. Palazzo Rondinini • Via del Corso 518
Mediocredito Centrale. Villino Casati • Via Piemonte 51
• Open: first Saturday of October
Admission free

Many Italians (and even more tourists) are unaware that for some years
various palaces now occupied by banks have been open to the public one
day each year. The open day is part of the *Invito a Palazzo* ["Invitation to
the Palace"] event organized by the Italian Banking Association (ABI).
The banks taking part in this initiative form a circuit of guided tours
through which lovers of hidden treasures of the arts can enjoy free
access to historic palaces, villas and gardens usually inaccessible to
the public.
The headquarters of the UniCredit Banca di Roma (Via del Corso)
possesses a curious oval spiral staircase built in 1713 for the Marchese
De Carolis by the famous Alessandro Specchi, architect of the palace
and spiritual heir of Borromini. The frescoes and canvases gracing the
first floor are the work of such artists as Giuseppe Bartolomeo Chiari,
Sebastiano Conca and Andrea Procaccini.
In Piazza del Gesù, the Altieri Palace (by the celebrated architect Giovanni
Antonio De Rossi), is also home to a number of masterpieces: the
ceiling of the headquarters of the Banca Finnat Euramerica is decorated
with a superb fresco by Canuti, *The Apotheosis of Romulus*, and that
of the ABI with a Maratta fresco, *The Triumph of Clemency*, while the
Banco Popolare's offices on the second floor are filled with sculptures,
tapestries, valuable pieces of furniture and a large collection of sacred
art, landscapes and scenes of everyday life.
BNL's head offices in Via Veneto were designed in the 1930s by the
architect Piacentinin and the building's halls are filled with antique
statues and a collection of paintings ranging from masterpieces by
Lotto and Canaletto to more modern canvases of Corot and Morandi.
Nor should the other banks be missed, including the Monte di Pietà
with its chapel (see p. 109), the headquarters of Banco di Sicilia in the
Mancini Palace, or the offices of Banca Antonveneta in Rondinini Palace
and the Mediocredito Centrale in the Casati Villa, former residence of the
socialite Marchesa Luisa Casati Stampa, well-known for her romantic and
intellectual relationship with the writer Gabriele D'Annunzio.

THE BOARDED-UP WINDOW AT PALAZZO MATTEI

Palazzo Mattei
19 Piazza Mattei

> *A room with no view*

There is a curious legend that Duke Mattei once lost a substantial part of his fortune. Hearing of this, his future father-in-law refused to give his daughter's hand in marriage.

So the duke decided to show the father that he had lost none of his power or noblesse, and overnight had the celebrated Fountain of the Turtles built in front of the palazzo.

The palazzo was part of what was known as the Mattei district, and today its façade still forms one of the sides of the pretty square of the same name. The next day, the duke invited his beautiful fiancée and her father to his palace to put matters right. He asked them to lean out of a little window from which there was a perfect view of the sumptuous fountain and declared: "Look what the unfortunate Duke Mattei can do in a few hours!"

The young woman's father offered his apologies and finally gave his approval to the marriage. As a souvenir of this memorable day, the duke had the window boarded up so that nobody else could appear at it. And you can still see it like that today.

The fountain was built around 1585 by the Florentine Taddeo Landini according to a design by Giacomo della Porta. It seems that on the original sketches the bronze ephebi were meant to be pushing dolphins in the upper basin, rather than the bronze turtles to which the fountain owes its name. These turtles, attributed to Bernini, were added later but have since been replaced by copies and the originals preserved in the Capitoline Museums.

WHY IS IT OFTEN WINDY IN PIAZZA DEL GESÙ?
Popular tradition holds that the square in front of the Jesuit Chiesa del Gesù is often very windy. According to a story told by Stendhal, one day the Wind, out walking with the Devil, came to the church of the Jesuits. The Devil, who had a mission to accomplish there, asked the Wind to wait for him a moment and went into the church. The Wind readily agreed, waiting one day, then two. Legend says it is still waiting there ...

CENTRE WEST

PRIVATE TOUR OF PALAZZO SACCHETTI

Via Giulia, 66
• Visits on request reserved for cultural associations or groups, Monday to Friday
Reservations: 06 68308950

> *A jewel waiting to be discovered*

The sumptuous Sacchetti Palace is still the residence of the family of that name, which explains why it is less famous than other Roman palaces, even though it was built and decorated by such renowned artists as Antonio da Sangallo and Francesco Salviati.

On the death of Sangallo, the original owner, the palace was bought by Cardinal Ricci di Montepulciano, who commissioned Nanni di Baccio Bigio to make some alterations, including the masterful Sala dei Mappamondi, with its walls frescoed by Salviati depicting scenes from the Old and New Testaments. The allegorical and mythological decorations of the majestic gallery were carried out by Giacomo Rocca.

In the middle of the 17th century, the palace passed into the hands of Cardinal Giulio Sacchetti, member of a family of Florentine merchants and bankers, who wasted no time in carving out a prominent position for himself in Roman society and acquiring the title of marquis, buying up vast properties in the Latium countryside and throwing himself enthusiastically into the business of artistic patronage.

Cardinal Giulio did not make many changes when he moved into this splendid palace, but he began to collect hundreds of precious objects, archaeological artefacts, and contemporary works of art, including some twenty paintings by Pietro da Cortona. Only two works remain from this remarkable collection, *Adam and Eve* and *The Holy Family*. The others have been dispersed, the fortunes of the Sacchetti family having sharply declined at the beginning of the 18th century following their dazzling rise up to the time of Cardinal Giulio, who at one point almost became pope.

At the side of the palace overlooking the Tiber, a recently restored nymphaeum still embellishes the garden, which used to run right down to the water before the construction of the quays. Within a small arcade are two niches with an ornamental basin and satyrs portrayed lifting a section of drapery to reveal an imaginary view of Rome. Above, the framed family coat of arms can be seen, surmounted by ephebes. In addition to the stucco, imitation marble, and mosaics, the artistic techniques used here are highly original: real shells embedded at various points alternate with festoons of fruit and flowers covered with coloured glass designs, not to mention the *tartari*, chalk formations imitating stalactites and stalagmites.

GONFALONE ORATORY

32/A Via del Gonfalone
• Tel: 06 6875952, 06 68805637, 06 9066572
• Bus: 23, 116, 116T, 271, 280, 870
• Opening times: During concerts, or on request

This small marvel of the16th century, hidden at the end of one of the many intersections of Via Giulia, once belonged to the important Archconfraternity of the Gonfalone. The oratory, which was restored between 1998 and 2002, remains almost unknown even though it is used today as a concert hall. It is however an extraordinary example of Roman Mannerism.

A little-known marvel

Although the building's small façade, by Domenico Castelli, is not particularly impressive, the interior is superb with its walls completely covered with an extraordinary cycle of frescoes featuring the Passion of Christ in twelve parts. They were painted in 1573 by Federico Zuccari, Livio Agresti, Cesare Nebbia, Bertoja, Raffaellino Da Reggio and Marco Pino. Wooden choir benches encircle the room. Also note the ceiling of carved and gilded wood, the work of Ambrogio Bonazzini dating from 1568.

Gonfalone means "standard" or "banner" and refers to the fact that, in the 14th century, Archconfraternity members used to raise the standard of the pope (who resided in Avignon at the time), as a sign of support for his sovereignty over Rome.

The confraternity, whose members wore a white habit and blue hood, was also known for the organisation of processions and other religious ceremonies. Their representations of Christ's Passion were so realistic that the popes had to put a stop to them in order to prevent crowd violence towards the Jews.

The Archconfraternity of the Gonfalone was dissolved at the end of the 19th century and the oratory fell into disuse, ending up in such a dilapidated state that it was used by refuse collectors as a storage area until a musician discovered this treasure and decided to use it as a concert hall.

CRIMINOLOGY MUSEUM

29 Via del Gonfalone
• Tel: 06 68300234
• Bus: 23, 116, 116T, 271, 280, 870
• Open Tuesday to Saturday, 9am-1pm, Tuesday and Thursday,
2:30pm-6:30pm
• Admission: €2

**Crime and
punishment**

This exceptional museum offers a detailed and fascinating reconstruction of the history of crime.

On the first floor, in the section devoted to the 19th century, studies of criminal anthropology, scientific police techniques, the history of the prison, the rise of judicial mental hospitals with restraint beds and straitjackets, are all presented. Then there are areas documenting political assassination attempts, various methods for identifying criminals, from fingerprinting to ID photos, and the history of criminal justice from the Middle Ages to the 19th century. This last section includes an impressive show of implements used to obtain confessions as well as instruments of every type for torture or capital punishment. Note the pillory or stocks, torture chair, whipping block, decapitation axe, and the sword of justice with which Beatrice Cenci was beheaded in 1599.

There are also plenty of whips and chains for punishing and transporting prisoners to hard labour camps.

On the second floor there is a display of finds from Italian prisons from the 1930s to the 1990s, evidence of perverse and criminal behaviour, such as espionage, organised crime (objects belonging to Salvatore Giuliano and Gaspare Pisciotta, Gennaro Cuocolo's ring, Pupetta Maresca's guns), terrorism, gambling and forgery of works of art.

Finally, a special area covers murders and news stories that caused a public stir in the 1940s and 1950s.

THE SECRET ROOMS OF SAINT PHILIP NERI ❹

Church of Santa Maria in Vallicella (Chiesa Nuova)
• Piazza della Chiesa Nuova
• Pre-booked guided tours Tuesdays, Thursday and Saturdays from
10am to 12pm
Duration: about 30 min
• E-mail: mauriziobotta@hotmail.com
• Tel.: 06 688 04695

> *Secrets of a saint unlike any other*

Three times a week, if you pre-book, you can get into the so-called "secret rooms of Saint Philip Neri". Although the rooms are not the historical site where the saint lived and prayed, the visit is still of great interest thanks to the enthusiastic personality of Father Maurizio Botta, a Filippini (from Filippo, the Italian name of the order's founder) who shows all the visitors round. You will also discover some particularly impressive aspects of the life of this saint, who is little known to the general public.

The tour begins in the red room, where a number of saintly relics are displayed as well as an attractive outline of the saint's standard (17th century) which the faithful carried during the seven churches pilgrimage. In the reproduction of Saint Philip's chapel, you can see a lovely Guercino painting, *The Vision of Saint Philip Neri*.

Notable works on the upper floor include a fine fresco by Pietro da Cortona (*The Ecstasy of Saint Philip*) and a Guido Reni painting of *Saint Philip Contemplating the Virgin*.

WHY DOES THE FAÇADE OF THE ORATORY OF SAINT PHILIP NERI CURVE INWARDS? Borromini's façade for the Filippini convent (notably the home of the oratory) was designed to be in harmony with the adjoining church. Its curve is reminiscent of the human body, arms outstretched, as if to welcome all those who cross its threshold.

The façade of the church of Santa Maria in Vallicella is embellished with statues of Saint Gregory to the left and Saint Jerome to the right. They are associated respectively with Pope Gregory XIII, who gave the church to Saint Philip, and the convent of San Girolamo della Carità (see page 115) where he spent many years.

SPIRITUAL CONCERTS IN CHIESA NUOVA SACRISTY
Once a month, from October to June, spiritual concerts in the revived tradition of Saint Philip Neri take place at 9pm in the superb sacristy of Chiesa Nuova. Admission is free, and pre-booking essential: padre.rocco@hotmail.com or musicaperduta@gmail.com. Entrance at 3 Via di Chiesa Nuova.

SAINT PHILIP NERI: A SAINT WHOSE HEART DOUBLED IN SIZE AS HE RECEIVED THE HOLY SPIRIT

Founder of the Congregation of the Oratory, also known as the Congregation of Filippinis after his forename, Saint Philip Neri (1515-1595) was often referred to as the joyful saint because of his cheerful disposition. Inspired by the early Christian communities, he wanted to anchor an intense spiritual life in daily routine based on prayer (he was one of the first to gather around him laymen with whom he prayed), reading, meditating on the word of God, and praising the Lord, mainly through chant and music. According to him, music was a special way of reaching people's hearts and bringing them to God (see article on the trapdoor in the Vallicelliana Library for listening to music from the oratory below, page 91). Thus he became one of the most avid defenders of the rebirth of sacred music. In 1544, while the saint was praying in the catacombs of Saint Sebastian over the tombs of the early martyrs, his heart was suddenly seized with immense joy and an intense light shone down on him. Raising his eyes, he saw a ball of fire which descended to his mouth and penetrated his chest. His heart, in contact with the flames, instantly dilated. The violence of the impact broke two of his ribs. The Holy Spirit had come to the saint, just as it had to the Apostles at Pentecost. In the 17th century, a scientific autopsy on his body confirmed that his was twice the size of any other human heart. Nothing was the same again for Saint Philip. The beating of his heart was so strong that it could be heard some distance away and the heat that constantly devoured him meant he could face the rigours of winter in his shirtsleeves. The symbol of the congregation today, a heart in flames, is based on this episode of his life. While looking after the sick, the poor and the infirm, he also took care to spend time with young people, wishing to stop them from falling into

boredom and depression. He often gathered a group around him and while always reminding them that life was to be lived joyfully, when the din became too loud one day, he is supposed to have said "Quieten down a bit, my friends, if you can"! His great spiritual gifts even enabled him to bring a child back to life for a few moments (see page 103).

SAINT PHILIP NERI AND THE PILGRIMAGE TO THE SEVEN CHURCHES OF ROME

Bringing the early pilgrimages to Rome to the tombs of Saint Paul and Saint Peter back into fashion, Saint Philip Neri and his followers began to visit the principal centres of worship in the city. Over time, these informal visits grew into a veritable pilgrimage around the seven major churches of Rome: San Pietro in Vaticano, San Paolo fuori le mura, San Sebastiano fuori le mura, San Giovanni in Laterano, Santa Croce in Gerusalemme, San Lorenzo fuori le mura and Santa Maria Maggiore. Each journey represented one of the seven stages of Christ's Passion. The pilgrimage still takes place today – enquire at Chiesa Nuova.

THE MOTORISED RUBENS

Church of Santa Maria in Vallicella (Chiesa Nuova)
Piazza della Chiesa Nuova
• Open in winter from 7:30am-12pm and 4:30pm-7:15pm (7:30pm in summer)
Masses in winter at 8am, 9am, 10am and 6:30pm (8am, 10am and 7pm in summer), Sundays at 10am, 11am, 12pm, 12:45pm, and 6:30pm (10am, 11am, 12pm and 7pm in summer)
• The Rubens painting slides down after the evening mass on Saturday and is raised again on Sunday evening after mass

Once a week, after the Saturday evening mass, Chiesa Nuova worshippers can take part in a very strange spectacle: the sexton lets down a Rubens painting by remote control to reveal a miraculous icon of the Virgin Mary behind it.

A painting that disappears once a week

The source of this phenomenon dates back to the early 16th century.

At that time, a fresco depicting the Virgin and Child was on view outside, on the façade of a public bathhouse where the apse of the church now stands. In 1535, an unbeliever threw a stone at the image of the Virgin, who astonishingly began to bleed. The image was placed inside the original Vallicella church for safekeeping. When the new church was built, following the installation of Saint Philip Neri's Congregation of the Oratory, the sacred image was in the first chapel to the right. But the conditions for conservation

of the fresco rapidly deteriorated and to safeguard it the decision was made to place it behind the high altar. In 1606, Rubens was commissioned to paint a canvas that would serve to protect the image of the Virgin.

A first attempt failed, but in 1608 Rubens produced a work entitled *Angels Adoring the Madonna Vallicelliana*, which incorporated a special feature – a panel that could be removed to reveal behind it the miraculous Holy image it was intended to protect.

MONUMENTAL HALL OF THE VALLICELLIANA ❻ LIBRARY

Piazza della Chiesa Nuova, 18
• To organise a free guided tour of the monumental hall and a programme of temporary exhibitions, e-mail the following address: b-vall.servizi@ beniculturali.it ; alternatively fax 06 6893868
• For further information contact Maria Teresa Erba on 06 68802671
• E-mail: mariateresa.erba@beniculturali.it
• Closed: 13-25 August and public holidays

A saint's library

Few people are familiar with the majestic monumental hall of the Biblioteca Vallicelliana, which forms part of the Institute of the Oratory of Saint Philip Neri (the Oratorians are a congregation of secular priests). On crossing the threshold, it is difficult not to fall under the spell of this vast rectangular chamber, the true dimensions of which are invisible from the outside, illuminated as it is by sixteen overhanging windows.

Decorated with stucco, wood panelling, and the monochrome canvases of G.B. Romanelli, the ceiling is exceptionally luminous. Spiral staircases have been concealed in the four corners of the hall to avoid breaking the homogeneity of the book-covered walls. The splendid wooden bookshelves dating from the 17th century are divided into two levels by a gallery supported by columns. The earliest documents relating to the order, founded by the Florentine priest Filippo (Philip) Neri in 1565, date back to 1581, but the growing number of adherents and the need for space to store the ever-increasing donations required an extension. Francesco Borromini carried out this work from 1637 to 1652. Following the rules of their order, the Oratorians attach great importance to books; each meal, for example, is accompanied by a reading or commentary on a sacred text. The library, originally made up of the personal collection of the founding saint, has been constantly enriched over the years to arrive at the present total of some 130,000 volumes, including rare manuscripts, incunabula, illustrated books and musical scores. Most texts are concerned with history or theology, but philosophy, law, botany, astronomy, architecture and medicine are also represented, and there is an exceptional collection of engravings and photographs.

THE LIBRARY TRAPDOOR
Saint Philip Neri asserted that music was a "fisher of souls" and the best form of spiritual diversion. Thus in the library there is a trapdoor that communicates with the oratory below, so that the music being played could be heard and inspire the readers above.

PICENI HOSPICE

15 Piazza San Salvatore in Lauro
• Open Mon-Fri 7:30am-1pm and 3:30pm-7pm, Sat 9am-12pm
and 4pm-8pm, Sun 9am-12pm

The Ospizio dei Piceni (Piceni Hospice), with its various buildings, courtyard, garden and cloister, is a practically unknown complex of extraordinary beauty.

A hidden cloister of unexpected beauty

Annexed to the much better known church of San Salvatore in Lauro, Piceni Hospice was one of the most important hospices in the city, where many people from the Marches region stayed when they came to Rome to live or simply to visit.

The Confraternity of the Piceni, who took over the church and adjacent monastic complex in 1669, for a long period offered assistance to people from their region.

The entrance is the via the church's first porch on the left. A few steps and you find yourself inside a spectacular 15th-century cloister with an overhead loggia. Beside the cloister is a small courtyard with a fountain and a beautiful portico that leads to the chapter house. Some important tombs such as that of Pope Eugene IV are also found here.

Apart from its historic importance and the artistic and architectural beauty that has been highlighted by long and careful restoration work, the hospice conceals another marvel.

On ascending the 16th-century staircase you can visit a superb place consisting of two vaulted rooms and a raised wing over the garden portico, with a beautiful trussed ceiling. It houses a museum donated by the painter Umberto Mastroianni, with over a hundred works dating back to his most significant and productive periods. The door next to the Mastroianni Museum is the entrance to the Emilio Greco Foundation.

The Pio Sodalizio dei Piceni foundation also organises exhibitions and musical and theatrical performances.

PALAZZO SCAPUCCI

18 Via dei Portoghesi
• Metro: A - Spagna or Barberini

***Monkey
business***

Palazzo Scapucci, which owes its name to the noble Roman family that owned it during the 16th and 17th centuries, encompasses a four-storey brick tower of medieval origin, restored on several occasions, with beautiful marble-framed windows. At its top, a strange statue will intrigue curious passers-by.

The tower owes its name to a legendary Roman anecdote, made famous by American novelist Nathaniel Hawthorne in *The Marble Faun*, according to which a pet monkey is supposed to have snatched the newborn son of the owners from his cradle and brought him to the top of the tower, jumping and playing dangerously amongst the battlements. It is said that the parents' desperate prayers to the Virgin Mary were heard (they promised to build a shrine in her honour if the child were saved) and the monkey brought him down safe and sound. The statue of the Virgin and the lamp at the top of the tower, both of which are visible from the street, date back to that time.

THE MORTET WORKSHOP

18 Via dei Portoghesi
• Metro: A - Spagna or Barberini
• Open Mon-Fri 9am-1pm and 3pm-6pm

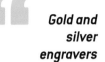

Gold and silver engravers

I t is well worth visiting the courtyard of the Scapucci palace to discover the fascinating Bottega Mortet (Mortet Workshop), belonging to the Mortet family who have been gold and silver engravers for over a century. The workshop is divided into various rooms, but its charm strikes you on entering the two rooms facing onto the courtyard. One of these, which is more like an office, is very welcoming and is used to receive customers. It has a display case, whereas the other room is the workshop properly speaking. Aurelio Mortet has been practising this old craft (which has almost disappeared in Rome) for over forty years with a passion handed down from generation to generation. His sons Dante and Andrea, and grandson Paolo, work together with great enthusiasm and welcome customers warmly. In Rome they are probably the only family who can boast such a rich and varied collection of products. In the hands of the Mortets gold and silver have taken on infinite shapes for often important customers, such as a gold pen for Pope John XXIII and a ring and cross for Pope Paul VI.

The reproductions of Roman fountains such as the *nasoni umbertini* (the typical nose-shaped Roman fountains) or the Fontana delle Tartarughe (Fountain of the Turtles) in Piazza Mattei are among the more original and fascinating pieces.

Their recent work includes producing the 2006 World Cup for the Italian football team.

TOUR OF THE ANGELICA LIBRARY

Piazza S. Agostino, 8
• Tel: 06 6840801 or 06 68408034 • E-mail: b-ange@beniculturali.it
• Director: Marina Panetta
• Group visits by arrangement or during exhibitions and concerts.
• Open Monday to Friday 8:30am-6:45pm and Saturday 8:30am-1:45pm
• Closed Sundays and the second and third weeks in August

> **Rome's oldest public library**

The Biblioteca Angelica is the oldest public library in Rome and one of the first to be founded in Europe. The ensemble has a rare beauty and the enigmatic atmosphere is so hushed that it gives the impression of going back in time.

Book lovers can enjoy these marvellous reading rooms and the precious manuscripts preserved herein during the exhibitions, concerts, and guided tours that are regularly organised.

The library is named after an Augustinian bishop, Angelo Rocca, who was in charge of the Vatican printing presses during the pontificate of Sixtus V and left his precious library to the brothers of the convent of Saint Augustine at the end of the 16th century. Rocca wanted anyone to be able to use the library – an outlandish idea at the time.

In 1661, Lukas Holste, then curator of the Vatican library, bequeathed his prodigious collection of printed volumes. In 1762, the acquisition of the books of Cardinal Domenico Passionei doubled this heritage, adding the works that the cardinal had personally acquired during his travels in Protestant countries. This explains why the library contains copies of forbidden texts, the importance of which has been crucial for understanding the Reformation and the Counter-Reformation.

It was around this time that the architect Luigi Vanvitelli was commissioned to restructure the library, particularly its spectacular reading room where scholars still gather today.

Over 200,000 volumes are preserved here, half of which were published between the 15th and the 18th centuries. The most important sections of the library are devoted to the history of the Reformation and the Counter-Reformation and to Augustinian thought, as well as to Dante, Petrarch and Boccaccio, theatre from the 15th to the 18th centuries, Italian and foreign journals of the 17th and 18th centuries, and works on Rome itself. This is also the location of rare books of great artistic value, notably a 9th-century manuscript of the Liber Memorialis from Remiremont Abbey in France, an illuminated codex to Dante's *Divine Comedy* dating from the 14th century, as well as two *mappemondes* (maps of the world) from 1603, the only ones in Italy.

Since 1940, the library has also been the headquarters of the Italian literary academy, or Accademia dell'Arcadia (see p. 151).

PALAZZO DELLA SAPIENZA AND ALEXANDRINE LIBRARY

⓫

Corso Rinascimento
• Pre-booked guided tours on the last Saturday of each month
• Tel: 06 68190895

> *A magnificent library open once a week*

Palazzo della Sapienza is open to the public on the last Saturday of the month. For centuries it was the monumental headquarters of the University of Rome "La Sapienza" (which moved to its current location in 1935), and is now home to the National Archives. The guided tour includes a general introduction to the history of the palace, as well as a visit to the courtyard, the study, where visitors are shown a number of historical documents, and the sumptuous Alexandrine Library, normally closed to the public. This library, established by Pope Alexander VII after whom it is named, is a vast rectangular hall divided into three aisles and surmounted by triple domed vaults. One of the interior walls features trompe-l'œil windows. The central vault is painted with a fresco representing the *Triumph of Religion*, a great allegorical work by Clemente Maioli.

The superb wooden shelving divided into two levels of stacks all around the walls was designed by Borromini between 1665 and 1669. A spiral staircase set in the middle of the west wall leads to a walkway round the upper stacks. There the shelves are topped with carved wooden motifs, like those of the arms of Alexander VII, whose marble bust, the work of Domenico Guidi, stands in an oval niche centred on one of the walls.

The building of the architectural complex consisting of palace, court and church took a long time, from the last quarter of the 16th century to the second half of the 17th century. Aesthetically, its remarkable success lies in the fusion of the austere Renaissance style of Giacomo della Porta with the Baroque dynamic of Francesco Borromini.

To the first of these men we owe the conception of the palace, whose rectangular form is arranged around a majestic courtyard surrounded with arcades on the ground floor and a loggia on three sides of the upper floor, while the fourth side unexpectedly closes off the ensemble with an exedra. Borromini, for his part, was responsible for the Alexandrine Library, the eastern façade of the palace near the church of Sant'Eustachio, and the spectacular church of Sant'Ivo alla Sapienza, using the form of Giacomo della Porta's simple but fundamental exedra as a façade abutted to his celebrated and inimitable dome with its corkscrew lantern.

PRIVATE TOUR OF PALAZZO PATRIZI

Piazza San Luigi dei Francesi
• By appointment only, contact Corso Patrizi Montoro
• Tel: 06 6869737 or 347 5476534

I f you prefer the secret charm of opulent private residences to museums, do not miss the Patrizi Palace in the Sant'Eustachio district (rione). The palace stands on land originally occupied by a simple building that was acquired by Giovanni Francesco Aldobrandini in 1596. Giacomo della Porta is probably the architect of the present facade, commissioned by Donna Olimpia Aldobrandini and built by Carlo Maderno.

> **The secrecy of private palaces**

The marquises of Patrizi, originally from Siena but related to noble Roman families, bought the palace in 1642 and had major alterations carried out, such as refurbishing the grand staircase under the direction of Gian Battista Mola, and the addition of a third storey, cornice, attic, and chapel. Two members of the family, Costanzo Patrizi (1589-1624) and Giovanni Battista Patrizi (1658-1727), were treasurers to the pope and keen patrons of the arts. It is to them that we owe most of the paintings in the family collection displayed in the rooms furnished with 17th- and 18th-century antiques, and in the dining room, where a splendid Meissen porcelain dinner service can also be seen.

The fact that it once included masterpieces such as Orazio Gentileschi's *Cupid and Psyche* (now in the Hermitage Museum, St Petersburg) or Caravaggio's *Supper at Emmaus* (now in the Brera Museum, Milan) gives a clear idea of the importance of the original collection, but several other remarkable works still remain at the palace.

The tour, with the master of the house as guide, covers the second floor – the historical residence of the Patrizi family – tracing their fortunes in papal Rome and giving a real sense of the past splendours of this luxurious dwelling.

DINNER FOR TWO IN THE PATRIZI PALACE
The Patrizi family, who still live in their eponymous palace, offer the possibility of hiring the premises for a romantic dinner.

THE PRIVATE CHAPEL OF PALAZZO MASSIMO ALLE COLONNE

141 Corso Vittorio Emanuele II
• Open once a year, 16 March, 7am-1pm

Commemorating a miracle by Saint Philip Neri

The private chapel of the Massimo family, dedicated to Saint Philip Neri in commemoration of one of his miracles, can only be visited once a year, on 16 March.

Paolo Massimo, the young son of Prince Fabrizio, died on 16 March 1583. Saint Philip was a friend of the family. Scarcely had he heard the news when he rushed to the boy's side to give him the last rites. He began to pray beside the body and the constant repetition of his name finally brought the boy round. The two spoke together, little Paolo claiming that he was happy to die because that would allow him to be reunited with his mother and sister in heaven. Saint Philip then placed his hand on the boy's head and said to him, "Go, with my blessing and pray to God for me". At these words, Paolo expired.

This story remained a secret until 1595, the year that Saint Philip was canonised, on the occasion of which Prince Fabrizio decided to reveal all. The miracle had taken place in the young boy's bedroom before it was converted into a chapel, which was restored and embellished over the centuries. Rectangular in shape, with a barrel vault, it contains eight marble columns supporting a decorated architrave, and three altars in polychrome marble. Pope Clement XI bequeathed the relics of Saint Clement the martyr to the main altar and in 1839, on the anniversary of the miracle, Gregory XVI promoted the chapel to the rank of church and opened it to the public once a year.

On that particular day, throughout the morning, the family allows people to go into the part of the palace housing the chapel. As the hours pass the few early morning habitués – close friends of the family or the saint's devotees – are replaced by a constant flow of curious visitors, fascinated and moved by the mysterious, reverential atmosphere characterising this ceremony, which is both intimate and solemn.

In the 16th century, the Massimo family owned three adjoining buildings, all of which are still standing today. The oldest of these is known as the Massimo Istoriato ("historiated" or illustrated) palace, because of the monochrome decorations of the Daniele da Volterra school gracing the façade overlooking Piazza de' Massimi. The Massimo di Pirro palace owes its name to a case of mistaken identity of a statue of Mars. The best known is however the Massimo alle Colonne, with its superb concave façade by Corso Vittorio, which Baldassarre Peruzzi built over the ruins of the *cavea* (tiered semicircular seating) of the Emperor Domitian's theatre.

THE STAIRCASE OF PALAZZO DEL GALLO DI ROCCAGIOVINE

⑭

Piazza Farnese

A scenic courtyard

This beautiful building, which often goes unnoticed because it stands opposite the much grander Palazzo Farnese, was constructed in 1520 by Baldassarre Peruzzi and has a magnificent staircase of a very distinctive design, which can be seen in the small interior courtyard.

On entering the building from Piazza Farnese through the main gate, walk into the courtyard and then turn around. You will see the palace's surprising main staircase. Opening onto the courtyard like a loggia, it climbs up three floors and has a gently sloping double ramp. It is decorated with columns, pilasters and a marble and stucco balustrade.

The building belonged to Ugo da Spina and then to Francesco Fusconi

da Norcia, before passing to the Pighini family, in whose hands it remained for over two centuries.

In 1720 the architect Alessandro Specchi was commissioned by the Pighinis to restore the building and it was he who designed the amazing staircase, based on a concept that was entirely new with respect to the traditional main staircase enclosed within a palace.

VINEGAR-MAKERS' ARCH

Via del Pellegrino, between numbers 19 and 41

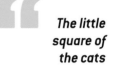

*The little
square of
the cats*

The name of Arco degli Acetari (Vinegar-Makers' Arch) probably comes from the former sellers of vinegar water (the Italian for "vinegar" being *aceto*).

Once through the small archway on Via del Pellegrino, you find yourself in a square in which time seems to have stood still. This courtyard is closed on four sides by picturesque houses that have kept their medieval look even today. It seems more like a country courtyard with all the cats sleeping on the steps, the flower-covered balconies and the wooden barrows.

The only access is through the archway. The traffic and pollution of Corso Vittorio and the hustle and bustle of Campo de' Fiori are just a stone's throw away, but seem quite distant.

REMAINS OF THE TEATRO DI POMPEO

The first and largest theatre ever built in Rome, inaugurated in the mid-1st century BC, has left many traces, even though most have been incorporated into the buildings superimposed on the site over the centuries.

The Theatre of Pompey was constructed by order of Gnaeus Pompeius Magnus, circumventing a law that prohibited the construction of permanent (non-wooden) theatres in the city: the great statesman thus had built, on an elevated podium, a temple dedicated to Venus Victrix and, opposite, an amphitheatre some 150 metres in diameter with rows of terraced seating (cavea) for spectators.

The semicircular form of the interior of the cavea can be clearly distinguished in the curved outlines of **Piazza dei Satir**i and **Via di Grottapinta**, while the exterior curves round from **Via del Biscione** to **Piazza Pollaiola**.

If you visit some of the shops on Via dei Giubbonari or go down into the cellars of the nearby buildings, you will discover parts of the substructure and the vaulting of the access ramps to the terraces.

Even more impressive archaeological remains can be seen on the lower floors of the restaurants *Da Pancrazio*, *Grotte del Teatro di Pompeo* and *Da Costanza*, as well as in the *Teatro di Pompeo* hotel, and inside the garage of the *Sole* hotel.

Da Pancrazio restaurant – 73 Via del Biscione
Grotte del Teatro di Pompeo restaurant – 92-94 Via del Biscione
Da Costanza restaurant – 63-65 Piazza del Paradiso
Teatro di Pompeo hotel – 8 Largo del Pallaro
Sole hotel – 76 Via del Biscione

THE MONTE DI PIETÀ CHAPEL

Piazza del Monte di Pietà
• Transport: Tram 8
• Opening times: Mornings for private visits. Advance reservation is
necessary by contacting Giovanni Innocenti by telephone at
06 67078495, or by fax at 06 67078112

*A hidden
Baroque
jewel*

Hidden behind a gate in the inner courtyard of the Palazzo del Monte di Pietà, this chapel covered in polychrome marble and stucco decorations is a jewel of Baroque architecture that remains almost unknown.

In 1639, the Monte di Pietà Archconfraternity commissioned Francesco Peperelli, an architect active in Rome during the first half of the 17th century, to carry out restructuring work on both the palace and the chapel. Giovanni Antonio de' Rossi took over from Peperelli, who died in 1641, and finished the work while respecting the original project.

On entering the small square atrium leading to the chapel, built between 1700 and 1702, one is struck by the beauty of the relief work by Michele Maglia in the centre of the oval-shaped vault, featuring the Eternal Father in Heaven surrounded by angels and garlands of flowers in golden stucco, by Andrea Berrettoni, Giovanni Maria Galli da Bibiena and Filippo Ferrari.

The atrium leads to the chapel, also oval-shaped. The gold stucco decorations and the shimmering colours of the marble covering the walls contrast with the white of the statues in their niches and the bas-reliefs on the altar and on the two side doors.

The statues representing the theological virtues *Faith, Hope and Charity* were the work of Francesco Moderati, Augusto Cornacchini and Giuseppe Mazzuoli respectively, and are accompanied by a contribution from Bernardino Cametti, symbolising *Alms* given by the confraternity to the needy. The extraordinary bas-relief on the altar is of a unique shape. It was created by Domenico Guidi in 1676 and it represents *Mercy*.

The two other beautiful bas-reliefs on the left and right sides of the altar represent *Tobias and the Angel*, a work by Pierre Le Gros, and *Joseph in Egypt*, by Jean-Baptiste Théodon.

The vault was decorated in 1696, based on a project by the architect Francesco Bizzacheri, with cornices, shells and plant ornaments in gilded stucco that join up with white stucco medallions by Michele Maglia, Lorenzo Ottoni and Simone Giorgini, depicting the main events surrounding the birth of the Monte di Pietà.

THE "NOBLE FLOOR" OF PALAZZO SPADA

13 Piazza Capo di Ferro
• Tel. 06 6832409
• Tram: 8
• Open the first Sunday of every month at 10:30am, 11:30am and 12:30pm
• Admission: €6 + entry ticket to Galleria Spada

> **A splendid palace open once a month**

Many curious passers-by go inside the courtyard of Palazzo Spada to admire the famous optical illusion created by Borromini, while lovers of 17th- and 18th-century paintings will have already contemplated those in the Spada Gallery, but very few also know of the palace's sumptuous *piano nobile* (literally "noble floor" in Italian – the main floor). The seat of the State Council, it is normally closed to the public except on the first Sunday of the month.

The palace, which was built at the behest of Cardinal Girolamo Capodiferro from 1548 onwards by the architect Bartolomeo Baronino, already had extraordinary paintings and stucco decorations decorating the Galleria degli Stucchi (Stucco Gallery) and the Sala delle Quattro Stagioni (Four Seasons Hall) of the main floor in 1550. Another extremely rich stucco decoration (by Giulio Mazzoni, Diego di Fiandra, Tommaso del Bosco and Leonardo Sormani) adorned the inner courtyard and the façade.

Cardinal Bernardino Spada acquired the palace in 1632, and commissioned painters, sculptors and architects with a series of new work. He extended the left wing of the palace onto Vicolo dell'Arco and the right wing onto Vicolo del Polverone, and created a painting gallery in four halls of the left wing of

the main floor (these halls have remained intact and today are open to the public), but above all he gave expression to his passion for optics and astronomy.

The walls of the Salone di Pompeo (Pompey Hall), next to the Four Seasons Hall, are painted with distorted architectural perspectives. The adjoining Corridor of the Meridian, a catoptric sundial based on reflected light and not on shadow, was constructed by Father Emmanuel Maignan (see below) in 1644 or 1646, depending on the source.

There is another catoptric sundial at the convent of Trinità dei Monti (see page 25 for more information on this type of sundial).

VENERABILE ARCICONFRATERNITA
DI
SANT'ANNA DE' PARAFRENIERI
IN S.CATERINA DELLA ROTA

DOMENICA
ORE 11.30
SANTA MESSA

CON LA PARTECIPAZIONE DEI CONFRATELLI

DOPO LA SANTA MESSA
SECONDO LA PLURISECOLARE TRADIZIONE
DI FRONTE ALL'ALTARE DI SANT'ANNA VERRA'
IMPARTITA LA BENEDIZIONE ALLE GESTANTI ED ALLE
PUERPERE CHE NE AVRANNO FATTO RICHIESTA

*

LA CHIESA DI S.CATERINA DELLA ROTA E' SEDE
DELL'ARCICONFRATENITA VATICANA

PER COMUNICAZIONI, SCRIVERE IMBUCANDO IN
VIA DI SAN GIROLAMO DELLA CARITA' N. 77

BLESSING OF EXPECTANT MOTHERS

Church of Santa Caterina della Rota - Piazza Santa Caterina della Rota
• The blessing of pregnant women takes place every Sunday after the
11:30am mass
• To take part, speak to the priest before the service starts

Have your unborn child blessed

Once a week, the church of Santa Caterina della Rota offers a blessing as unusual as it is moving. After the 11:30 mass on Sunday mornings, in a solemn candle-lit atmosphere and in the presence of monks and nuns, expectant mothers can have a blessing bestowed on them by a priest from the Archconfraternity of Pontifical Grooms before the altar dedicated to Saint Anne, mother of the Blessed Virgin. Mothers who have recently given birth are also welcome.

Santa Caterina della Rota church became the Confraternity's headquarters in 1929, following a decree by Pius XI. The church of Sant'Anna dei Palafrenieri

(in Vatican City, behind Porta Angelica), where the Confraternity had been based for centuries, had become a parish of the Vatican.

To the left of the altar you will see two curious red uniforms. These belong to the bearers of the *sedia gestatoria* (gestatorial chair) on which popes used to be carried during certain ceremonies. These chair-bearers are now in the service of the pontifical household when the Holy Father gives audiences. Their Confraternity merged with the Grooms when the latter's equestrian team was abolished.

VENERABILE ARCICONFRATERNITA DI SANT'ANNA DE PARAFRENIERI

The Archconfraternity of Pontifical Grooms was established in 1378 at the request of Urban VI. The role of the Grooms, whose Italian name comes from *palafreno* (palfrey), a breed of horse popular for ceremonial use, was similar to that of equerries at court. They served the pope, who protected them and to whom they were very close. Over time, they acquired a number of material and spiritual privileges. Notably, they had the power to grant titles of doctor of theology or of letters, legitimise children born out of wedlock and absolve criminals from any penalty, even that of death.

CARAVAGGIO'S *OUR LADY OF THE GROOMS*

In the 17th century, the Archconfraternity of Pontifical Grooms commissioned Caravaggio to paint a picture of Saint Anne with the Virgin and Child. Completed in 1606, it was rejected for being too "unseemly". Cardinal Scipione Borghese acquired the painting, now renowned as Our Lady of the Grooms. It can be seen at the Museo e Galleria Borghese.

CAPPELLA SPADA

San Girolamo della Carità
62 Via Monserrato
• Access from Piazza Santa Caterina della Rota
• Open Sundays 10:30am-12:30pm

> **Pivoting angel's wings lead to a little-known masterpiece**

Near Piazza Farnese, the church of San Girolamo della Carità is home to an unusual and little-known masterpiece of Baroque art, long attributed to Borromini.

The Spada chapel is the first on the right on entering the church by the main portal. It was decorated at the request of an influential Oratorian,* Virgilio Spada, who probably commissioned the architect Francesco Righi.

This chapel, whose originality lies in its superb polychrome marble, is separated from the church by a remarkable balustrade designed by Antonio Giorgetti, a pupil of Bernini. It consists of two statues of kneeling angels holding up a great sheet of jasper. Their wings are of wood, and those on the right pivot on hinges to allow access to the chapel. There is not much of note architecturally, but mosaic lovers will be enchanted by the interior. The veined jasper and precious marble suggest damask cloth embroidered with flowers, acanthus leaves, lilies, stars and swords, as if flowing over the floor and the smooth walls of the chapel. The last three of these motifs (lily, star and sword) are the symbols of the Spada family (*spada* being Italian for sword).

On either side of the altar (a simple block also decorated with mosaics of precious marble), are statues of Bernardino Spada (by Ercole Ferrata) and Giovanni Spada (by Cosimo Fancelli) recumbent on their respective tombs

Tradition has it that this church was built on the very spot where the house of the widow Paula (who, in the 4th century AD, gave shelter to Saint Jerome) once stood. This was the house that Domenico Castelli rebuilt around the mid-17th century.

Before leaving the church, do not overlook the small and beautiful Antamoro chapel to the left of the high altar, the only work in Rome by Filippo Juvarra, and the statue of Saint Philip Neri by Pierre Legros.

SAINT PHILIP NERI'S CELL AT SAN GIROLAMO DELLA CARITÀ
Saint Philip lived for some thirty years in the convent of San Girolamo della Carità (an annex of the church). His cell, which has been turned into a chapel, can still be seen. To book a visit, call 06 6879786.

*Member of the Congregation of Saint Philip Neri

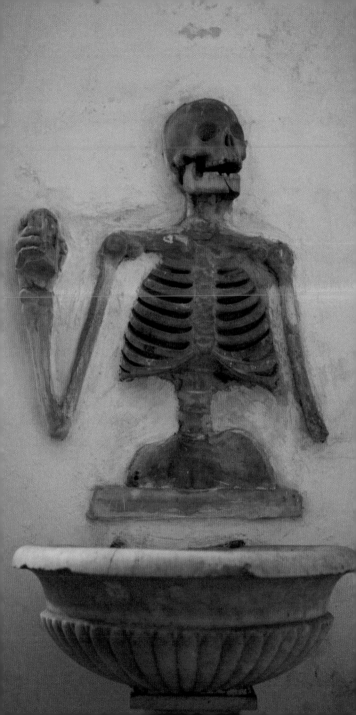

HYPOGEUM CEMETERY OF SANTA MARIA DELL'ORAZIONE E MORTE CHURCH

⓴

262 Via Giulia
- Daily tours, 4pm-6pm; Sundays, 4pm-7pm
- E-mail: billa.sapia@tiscali.it

"My turn today, yours tomorrow"

The church of Santa Maria dell'Orazione e Morte, seat of the arch brotherhood of the same name, overlooks Via Giulia opposite the Farnese arch. The façade bears a plaque featuring a skeleton who warns passers-by: *Hodie mihi, cras tibi* (literally, "Today for me, tomorrow for you").

Inside, having noted the decorations rich in necrological symbols, you enter the crypt via the sacristy, to the left of the master altar: you can also visit the remains of the ancient cemetery, the greater part of which was destroyed around 1870 during the construction of the barrier walls along the Tiber, the river waters having flooded the cells on more than one occasion. Two plaques still indicate the different levels that the water had reached inside the cemetery.

From 1552 to 1896, the brotherhood gathered over 8,000 bodies, a fair number of which were buried in this crypt. Wherever a body was found without a grave, in the depths of a bog, thrown up by the Tiber or the sea, or lying in the brush, the members of the brotherhood would recover it for holy burial.

Today, these galleries are like a boneyard in which the decorative artwork, crosses, sculptures and lamps have been made from bones and skeletons. In addition, the name of the deceased has been engraved on certain exposed skulls, with the date and sometimes the cause of death together with the place where the body was found.

THE VATICAN & SURROUNDING AREA

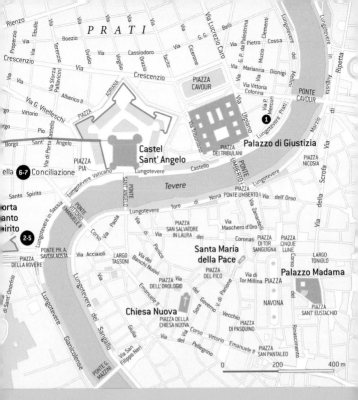

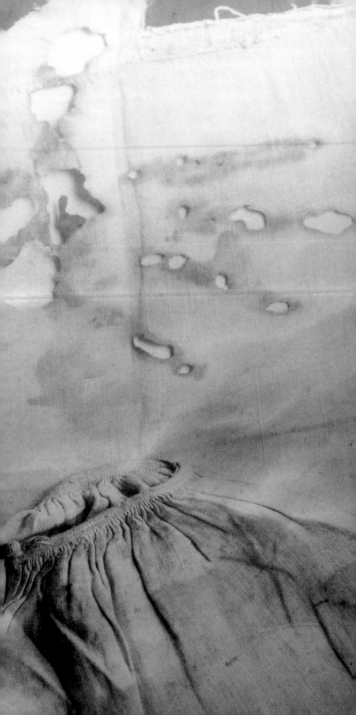

MUSEUM OF THE SOULS IN PURGATORY

12 Lungotevere Prati
- Tel: 06 68806517
- 7.30am-11am, 4pm-7pm
- Admission free

Traces of the netherworld

The church of the Sacro Cuore del Suffragio (Sacred Heart of Suffrage) was built at the behest of father Victor Jouet, a French priest from Marseilles, who acquired a large plot of building land in Lungotevere Prati in 1893. The peculiarity of this building, which was designed by Giuseppe Gualandi, is that it is entirely built in Gothic style, so much so that some have called it the "small dome of Milan".

In 1897 a fire broke out in a chapel that no longer exists, dedicated to Our Lady of the Rosary, and when the fire was extinguished, faithful bystanders noticed that on one side of the altar there was the image of a face, which, it was said, belonged to a soul in Purgatory. This amazing event prompted Father Jouet to try to find other testimonies concerning the souls in Purgatory. The result of his research is the collection that is preserved today in a showcase hanging on the wall of a small corridor leading to the sacristy.

The collection consists of about a dozen disturbing relics in the form of writing material, fabrics, books and photos that testify to presumed contact between the living and souls in Purgatory. These signs have been left by the souls of the deceased asking for prayers and indulgence.

The relics found here are quite enigmatic: the imprint of three fingers left in 1871 on Maria Zaganti's book of devotion by the deceased Palmira Rastelli who was asking for a holy mass to be said for her, the photo of an imprint by the deceased Mrs Leleux burned into the sleeve of her son Giuseppe's shirt during her apparition in 1789 in Wodecq in Belgium, the burned imprint of Sister Maria di San Luigi Gonzaga's finger when she appeared to Sister Maria of the Sacred Heart in 1894, and finally the imprint left on Margherita Demmerlè's book by her mother-in-law who appeared 30 years after her death, in the parish of Ellinghen in 1815.

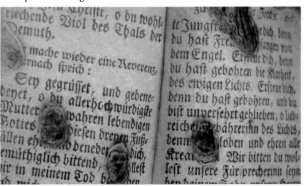

NATIONAL MUSEUM OF THE HISTORY OF MEDICINE

3 Lungotevere in Sassia
• Tel: 06 68352353
• From September to June, Monday, Wednesday and Friday 10am-12pm

> *A little museum of horrors*

The museum, which was planned after the First World War to bring together medical material collected for the 1911 World Fair, was opened in 1933 in nine large rooms at the Pio Istituto di Santo Spirito (Pious Institute of the Holy Spirit). There is no other museum in Italy with as many artefacts relating to the history of medicine as this one.

The visit starts in the Sala Alessandrina on the ground floor, with hand-painted anatomical tables from the 17th and 18th centuries hanging on the walls.

The Sala Flaiani contains the remains of one of the most important anatomical museums of Europe, the Museo di Santo Spirito (Museum of the Holy Spirit), founded in the 18th century by the great surgeon Flaiani. Here one can observe several anatomical preparations that have been kept unaltered over the centuries thanks to refined preservation techniques. These include skeletal alterations, examples of pathological anatomy, deformed foetuses, skulls and limbs affected by syphilis and mummified heads. In the centre of the room there is a mill in the form of a wooden temple, which was used to grind quinine.

The next hall is the Sala Capparoni, where a series of incredibly realistic Roman and Etruscan ex voto offerings are preserved along with other modern wax ex voto offerings, as well as a collection of Roman, medieval, Renaissance and 19th-century surgical instruments, and a phial of scorpion oil for poisonous animal bites and stings. There are also some snakes' tongues, a crown used for headaches, Renaissance first-aid kits, a collection of glass and ceramic recipients used to keep medicines and a 19th-century electrotherapy machine.

The Sala Carbonelli today houses fascinating and macabre objects and instruments: a collection of drills, saws for amputating from the 16th to the 19th centuries, anal and vaginal specula from the 15th to the 19th centuries, microscopes and glasses of all shapes and from all periods, the two glass beakers used by Avogadro to demonstrate the law of the compression of gases, a girl's hand metallised by a process that is still unknown, a huge wooden 17th-century press for extracting plant essences, and some stone and metal mortars for making medicinal potions. The reconstructions of an old pharmacy and the chemical-alchemical laboratory from the 17th century are beautiful. You can also admire a 16th-century walnut bookcase with over ten thousand books, prints and reviews concerning the history of medicine on its shelves.

MONUMENTAL COMPLEX OF SANTO SPIRITO IN SASSIA

1-2-3 Borgo Santo Spirito
• Individual guided tours Mondays at 10am and 3:30pm
• Reservations for group tours with qualified guide: 06 68352433 or 06 68210854

> *Rare visit to a former hospital*

Once a week, the remarkable architectural ensemble of Santo Spirito in Sassia is open to visitors.

On the initiative of the King of Wessex, the "Schola Sacorum" (Saxon School), a charitable institution for Saxon pilgrims on their way to visit Saint Peter's tomb in Rome, was created in the 8th century. The buildings, later destroyed by fire and pillaging, were reconstructed at the end of the 12th century on the orders of Pope Innocent III, who dedicated the main section to helping the sick, paupers and abandoned babies. Under the name Santo Spirito in Sassia, it grew into the most advanced hospital of its time. The grand rectangular gallery could receive up to a thousand people.

The tour begins in the Corsia Sistina (Sistine Ward), which Pope Sixtus IV added to the hospital two centuries later. The gallery, 120 metres in length and 13 metres high, is divided into two sections by a majestic tiburium, in the centre of which rises a very beautiful altar, the only work by Palladio to be found in Rome. The interior portal, finely carved in marble and attributed to Andrea Bregno, is called the Portale del Paradiso (Heaven's Door). Next to this entrance is the "foundlings' wheel" (see page 129). Sixtus IV had the walls of this gallery frescoed to the level of the windows to celebrate the establishment of the hospital and the merits of Innocent III, as well as for his own glory. He also ordered the construction of two buildings adjoining the superb cloisters, reserved respectively for the monks and nuns who worked at the institute (at present, only the priest's quarters are open to the public).

Around 1570, Monseigneur Cirillo, then Commander of the brotherhood, enlarged the hospital by building the Palazzo del Commendatore around a splendid courtyard. A grand staircase leads to the upper gallery where frescoes by Ercole Perillo entirely cover the upper part of the walls. This gallery leads into the Lancisiana library (18th century, currently under restoration), and the Commander's former apartment, decorated with sculptures, tapestries, antique furniture and frescoes by Jacopo and Francesco Zucchi telling the story of the hospital.

THE ITALIAN CLOCK OF THE PALAZZO DEL COMMENDATORE ❹

Via Borgo di Santo Spirito, 3

> *A clock with only six hours*

A huge and unusual clock dominates the courtyard of the former Santo Spirito architectural ensemble, set in the cornice of the Palazzo del Commendatore (Palace of the Commander, as the president of the charitable institution of Santo Spirito used to be known).

This curious Baroque clock dates back to 1828 and has the particularity of possessing an "Italian" face, divided into six sections (see below). The clock face is encircled by a serpent biting its own tail, while a bronze lizard (symbol of death and resurrection) takes the place of a hand.

WHAT IS THE ORIGIN OF "ITALIAN" CLOCKS?

The subdivision of the day into hours goes back to antiquity and was probably introduced by the Chaldeans. Whereas the Babylonians and Chinese measured time in double hours, twelve *kaspars* a day for the former and twelve *tokis* for the latter, the Greeks and Romans divided the day into two equal parts of twelve hours each. As the time from sunrise to sunset varied with the season, daylight hours in summer were longer than the hours of darkness, while the reverse held true in winter.

The rigorous discipline of monastic orders, especially the Benedictines, led to a radical upheaval in ways of measuring time. The hour began to be calculated by sundials that did not show the hour, but the religious duty to be fulfilled at various moments of day and night (matins, vespers, etc.). At the end of the 13th century, mechanical clocks made their appearance in Europe. This was a true revolution, as from then on the hour had a fixed duration, to such an extent that by the end of the 14th century most towns had abandoned the solar hour indicated by a gnomon to organise themselves by the striking of the church tower clock.

The day began at sunset and was divided into twenty-four hours: consequently the clock faces were graduated from I to XXIV. However people soon got tired of counting twenty-four chimes, not to mention the innumerable errors that occurred.

So from the 15th century the system was modified so that the clock would strike only six times a day instead of twenty-four. Little time was wasted in applying this simplification and so clock faces began to be numbered I to VI, like that of San Niccolò castle. During the Napoleonic campaigns, "Italian" time was replaced by "French-style" time, where clocks were numbered I to XII and the day started at midnight.

THE FOUNDLINGS' WHEEL

Former hospital of Santo Spirito in Sassia
Borgo Santo Spirito
• Guided tours Mondays at 10am and 3pm

Backing onto the right-hand side of the Santo Spirito in Sassia complex, you can still see today a small construction fitted with a grille through which can be glimpsed a "foundlings' wheel" intended to discreetly receive unwanted newborn infants (see below).

For abandoning your child discreetly

Before these wheels existed, the most common practice was "oblation" (offering to God), which was not considered abandonment since the parents "gave" their child to a convent that not only welcomed it but offered it a place in monastic life.

In Italy, the first wheel was installed at this hospital by Pope Innocent III in 1198. In the second half of the 19th century there were 1,200 "wheels" of this kind in Italy, but they were abolished from 1867 and finally disappeared in 1923.

WHAT IS A FOUNDLINGS' WHEEL?

It is said that in 787, Dateus, a priest in Milan, began placing a large basket outside his church so that abandoned infants could be left there. More organised initiatives for the reception of abandoned children were begun by the Hospice des Chanoines in Marseilles from 1188 onwards, with Pope Innocent III (1198-1216) later giving the practice the Church's benediction; he had been horrified by the terrible sight of the bodies of abandoned infants floating in the Tiber and was determined to do something to save them.

So the doors of convents were equipped with a sort of rotating cradle which made it possible for parents to leave their infant anonymously and without exposing it to the elements. The infant was left in the outside section of the cradle, and then the parent rang a bell so that the nuns could activate the mechanism and bring the child inside. Access to the "turntable" was, however, protected by a grille so narrow that only newborn infants would fit through...

Abandoned during the 19th century, the system had to be readopted after some twenty years at various places in Europe due to the sharp upturn in the number of infants abandoned.

You can see historic foundling wheels at the Vatican, Pisa and Florence (see the *Secret Tuscany* guide from the same publisher), in Bayonne and in Barcelona (see the *Secret Barcelona* guide).

HEADQUARTERS OF THE ORDER OF THE HOLY SEPULCHRE

6

Palazzo della Rovere - Via della Conciliazione, 33
• For a guided tour of the Order's international headquarters: 06 0877347

> *A palace so beautiful that Charles VIII preferred it to the Vatican ...*

Since 1950, Hotel Columbus has occupied a wing of the Palazzo della Rovere, a magnificent 15th-century residence belonging to the Equestrian Order of the Holy Sepulchre of Jerusalem, where some little-known treasures are to be discovered. The five sumptuous rooms of the *piano nobile* (high-ceilinged main floor) house the administrative offices of the Order, but they can be toured in the company of a guide, booked in advance. Between 1480 and 1490, Cardinal Domenico della Rovere, nephew of Pope Sixtus IV, commissioned architect Baccio Pontelli to build this prodigious edifice on the narrow street that led from Saint Peter's Basilica to the Castel Sant'Angelo (Mausoleum of Hadrian). The decoration was carried out by the most celebrated artists of the time. It is said that this palace was so beautiful that Charles VIII preferred to stay there rather than at the Vatican. Several cardinals in their turn chose to live there until 1655, when the palace was bought by the Order of the Penitentiaries (a religious order charged with hearing the confessions of pilgrims who presented themselves at the basilica), which would remain there for the next 300 years. Looking out from the former doorway, two small 17th-century fountains can be seen, one adorned with an eagle and the other bearing the dragon of the Borghese family. The façade is known to have been decorated with 16th-century graffiti, now eroded by the ravages of time. The *piano nobile* opens onto a succession of rooms decorated by Pinturicchio and other painters of his school: the Hall of the Grand Master, the Hall of the Seasons or the Zodiac, the Hall of the Prophets and the Apostles, and finally the Hall of the Demigods, in perfect condition, with a superb wooden ceiling featuring figures painted on sheets of paper fixed to the beams. Pheasants peck at the ears of wheat under the English oak, the coat of arms of the Della Rovere, resplendent in the centre and at the four corners of the ceiling. Cardinal Alidosi had the chapel added in 1505. It is fitted with a beamed vault adorned with eagle and oak tree, the motifs of which are repeated, with the following motto: "Profit, O mortals, from your leisure, enlivened by nourishment in the shade of the oak". On the second floor of the hotel wing there are two rooms with frescoed ceilings commissioned by Cardinal Giovanni Salviati and painted by Francesco Salviati.

WHERE TO EAT NEARBY

RESTAURANT *LA VERANDA*

7

Borgo Santo Spirito, 73 • Tel. : 06 6872973

To appreciate the Palazzo della Rovere without staying at Hotel Columbus or visiting it, you can have a drink or dine at the Veranda restaurant, within the hotel. Whether seated in the garden or below the painted vaulted ceilings, the atmosphere is particularly romantic at night.

SAINT PETER'S MERIDIAN

Piazza San Pietro

8

A forgotten giant sundial

Since 1817, the famous obelisk of Saint Peter's Square – a red granite monolith over 25 metres high, or 40 metres if you count the base and the cross – is one of the world's largest gnomons marking a meridian (see the Place de la Concorde meridian in *Secret Paris*, in this series of guides). On the paving stones of the square is a strip of granite that forms a straight line linking a point to the right of the base of the obelisk to another point beyond the Maderno fountain.

At each end of this strip, two marble discs indicate the points where, at midday, the shadow of the cross is projected during the summer solstice (in the sign of Cancer) and the winter solstice (in the sign of Capricorn). Five more discs mark the passage of the sun through the other signs of the zodiac, arranged in pairs: Leo-Gemini, Virgo-Taurus, Libra-Aries, Scorpio-Pisces and Sagittarius-Aquarius.

The obelisk was probably erected at Heliopolis during the 12th dynasty (20th-18th centuries BC). Caligula had it brought to Rome in AD 37 to set off his private circus, on the Vatican hill, before it was taken over by Nero.

Several popes have attempted to embellish or otherwise make their mark on the obelisk. Sixtus V, for example, decided to add four lions to the base as a reference to the coat of arms of his family, the Peretti, and he donated the bronze ball that surmounts the obelisk, claimed to contain the ashes of Caesar,

to the municipality of Rome. Alexander VII crowned it with the Chigi symbols of mountains and stars, and Innocent XIII added the bronze eagles and the heraldic emblems of the Conti family.

The obelisk of Saint Peter's Square is the only one in Rome not to have collapsed. It even remained in its original position beside the basilica until 1586, when Sixtus V asked Domenico Fontana to move it to its present site.

SANCTVS
LONGINVS
MARTYR

THE LONGINUS LANCE AT SAINT PETER'S

Saint Peter's Basilica
• Open daily, 7am-7pm from April to October, and 7am-6pm from
November to March

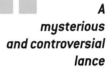

A mysterious and controversial lance

I n front of Bernini's baldachin, to the left seen from the church entrance, there is another statue by Bernini, in a similar style to the statue of Veronica (see p. 137), representing Saint Longinus in the act of piercing the side of Christ on the Cross.

Although the church treasury possesses a fragment of this lance, the location where the main section is preserved is a closely guarded secret.

THE LANCE THAT PIERCED THE SIDE OF CHRIST ON THE CROSS: A FERVENTLY DISPUTED RELIC

According to the Gospel of Saint John, a Roman soldier pierced the side of Jesus with a lance to ensure that he was dead. Blood flowed from the wound, a symbol of his sacrifice, as did water, a symbol of his fecundity. Some also read into this scene the birth of the Church from the body of Christ, just as Eve had sprung from Adam's rib.

The apocryphal Gospel of Nicodemus (circa 450 AD) adds a detail: the name of the soldier was Longinus, as shown by a miniature in a manuscript of the Laurentian Library at Florence, even though some believe that the name in Greek characters (ΛΟΓΙΝΟC), or LOGINOS, was simply derived from the word for "lance". Tradition says that Longinus, partially blind, was also touched by a drop of Christ's blood and water, which immediately restored his sight. The retrieval of this lance, not mentioned by the other evangelists, has been the object of intense competition to acquire such an important relic. Apparently taken to Constantinople in 615 to escape from the sack of Jerusalem by the Persians, the lance probably remained there until 1244, when it was presented to Saint Louis (the French king Louis IX) by the emperor Baldwin II together with Jesus' crown of thorns, which is still preserved in Notre-Dame Cathedral in Paris (see *Secret Paris* in this series of guides). The lance was later transferred to the Bibliothèque Nationale during the French Revolution and then disappeared. Note that meanwhile several copies have appeared: one has been spotted in Jerusalem, another in Constantinople and yet others are to be found in Cracow, Vienna, Budapest and Ejmiadzin in Armenia. The Armenian lance was said to have been recovered during the First Crusade: in 1098, a certain Pierre Barthelemy had a vision in which Saint Andrew showed him that the lance was in Saint Peter's Church at Antioch. The crusaders captured Antioch, found the lance in the predicted place, and then carried it off to Armenia.

THE VEIL OF VERONICA AT SAINT PETER'S ❿

Saint Peter's Basilica
• Open daily, 7am-7pm from April to October, and 7am-6pm from
November to March

"

V ery few visitors to Saint Peter's pay much attention to the statues around Bernini's baldachin in the central space of the basilica. Behind it, on the left (as seen from the entrance), is displayed a statue of Veronica, whose extraordinary history is virtually unknown. Above the statue is preserved her original veil (see box).

A little-known rival to the Shroud of Turin?

THE EXTRAORDINARY SAGA OF VERONICA'S VEIL

A great many churches possess a copy of a veil on which is imprinted the miraculous image of the face of Christ. The origin of this image is to be found in the Gospels of Mark (5: 25-34), Matthew (9: 20-22) and Luke (8: 43-48), which all relate the story of a woman who was healed of a haemorrhage by Jesus. Around the year 400, the Bishop of Lydia named her Berenike, a little before the apocryphal Gospel of Nicodemus (circa 450) finally referred to her as Veronica. The name seems to derive from "vero" and "icona", meaning "true image", while the personality of Veronica was embellished, gradually departing from the miraculously healed woman. In the 7th century, another apocryphal text, The Death of Pilate, spoke of Veronica as a confidante of Jesus to whom he had given the veil on which his face was imprinted.

Towards 1160, the canon of Saint Peter's Basilica in Rome, Pietro Mallius, put forward the hypothesis that this legend had arisen when, seeing Christ carrying his Cross to Golgotha, a woman removed her veil to wipe his brow and the image of his face was miraculously imprinted on it. This notion took root and little by little it was established as the true version of this rare and miraculous acheiropoieta (an image not made by the hand of man) (see p. 141).

Still according to legend, Veronica's veil was first reported to be kept in Saint Peter's Basilica in 1287, although Pope Celestine III (1191-1198) had previously mentioned the existence of such a shroud. The veil may have been sold during the sack of Rome in 1527, but, as often happens with relics, it soon reappeared and was again noted in the relics hall in the 17th century, although some claimed that the face imprinted on the veil was that of a peasant named Manopello.

The cathedral of Jaen, in Spain, also claim to possess the authentic veil of Veronica.

THE CULT OF CHRISTIAN RELICS

Although rather neglected these days, with their devoted following greatly diminished in numbers, saints' relics had extraordinary success from the Middle Ages onwards. Their presence today in numerous churches across Europe is a reminder of those exceptional times.

The cult of Christian relics goes back to the beginning of Christianity, to the deaths of the early martyrs and the creation of the first saints. The function of these relics was threefold: they bore witness to the example of a righteous and virtuous life to be copied or followed; they possessed a spiritual energy and power that could even work miracles (it was believed that the miraculous powers of the saints themselves was retained by their relics); and over time, with the rise of the contested practice of granting indulgences, relics bestowed indulgences on those who possessed them (see page 145).

As demand dictated supply, it was not long before unscrupulous parties were competing to invent their own relics, aided in their task by the Church which, for political reasons, canonised a great number of undeserving individuals (see opposite). Over-production went to absurd extremes: if one accepted the authenticity of all their relics, Mary Magdalene would have had six bodies, and St Biagio a hundred arms.

These excesses, of course, raised suspicions and the popularity of relics gradually waned, although many people still believe that the true relic of a saint possesses spiritual power. How else can one explain the numerous pilgrimages in the footsteps of Father Pio throughout Italy?

There are around 50,000 relics scattered around Europe, from some 5,000 saints.

Note that most of the world's other religions also worship relics, or used to do so.

21,441 RELICS FOR 39,924,120 YEARS OF INDULGENCES! The greatest collector of relics was Frederick III of Saxony (1463-1525), who procured 21,441 of them in all, 42 of which were fully preserved bodies of saints. Based on this unique collection, he calculated that he had amassed a grand total of 39,924,120 years and 220 days of indulgences! However, under the influence of Luther, who opposed indulgences, he abandoned the cult of relics in 1523.

WHEN SAINTS ARE NOT SO HOLY: SAINT GEORGE, SAINT CHRISTOPHER, AND SAINT PHILOMENA, STRUCK FROM THE LIST...

From the Middle Ages onwards, the pursuit of relics continued, as did their falsification. Not only relics were fabricated, however. Sometimes, even the saints themselves were a fabrication.

Recently – an event that passed almost without comment – the Church purged Saint George, Saint Christopher and Saint Philomena from its calendar, the very existence of all three now being in doubt.

The totally abusive canonisation of certain real personalities also took place, allowing the objects connected with them to feed the market for saintly relics.

For diplomatic reasons linked to the Counter-Reformation of the 16th century, canonisation was often based on political rather than religious or moral criteria. As a result of this *Realpolitik*, many rulers of the time were thus sanctified in a bid to ensure their subjects' allegiance to the Roman Catholic Church, then under pressure from the Protestant movement. Saint Stanislas of Poland, Saint Casimir of Lithuania, Saint Brigitte of Sweden, Saint Stephen of Hungary, Saint Margaret of Scotland, Saint Elizabeth of Portugal, Saint Wenceslas of Bohemia ... The list is long, indeed.

RELICS OF THE FEATHERS OF THE ARCHANGEL MICHAEL, THE BREATH OF JESUS, AND EVEN THE STARLIGHT THAT GUIDED THE THREE WISE MEN!

Leaving no stone unturned in their efforts to make money at the expense of the most naive believers, relic merchants showed unparalleled imagination in their quest for sacred paraphernalia and invented some fascinating objects, such as the horns of Moses or the feathers of the Archangel Michael, recorded as having been on sale at Mont-Saint-Michel in 1784.

The most highly prized relics were of course those of Christ. Unfortunately for relic hunters, as Christ had ascended to Heaven, his body was by definition no longer on Earth. Imagination again came to the rescue in the form of the quite extraordinary relic of the breath of Jesus (!) which was preserved in Wittenberg cathedral, Germany, in a glass phial.

The remains of Christ's foreskin, recuperated after his circumcision seven days after birth, and of his umbilical cord (!) were preserved at Latran, Rome (in the Sancta Sanctorum) while bread from the Last Supper was kept at Gaming, Austria. Certain medieval texts lost to us today even spoke of the relic of the rays of the star that guided the Wise Men, also preserved at Latran.

ACHEIROPOIETIC WORKS OF ART

In Christian doctrine the Greek term *acheiropoieta* is used to describe works of art "not made by human hands". Although these artefacts are relatively rare, some can nevertheless be seen, for example at the legendary but mysterious Mount Athos in Greece. This semi-autonomous republic of Orthodox monks, isolated on a peninsula in north-eastern Greece and forbidden to women, children and female animals since the 11th century, is home to two acheiropoietic icons. One is kept at the Holy Monastery of Megisti Lavra, the other at the Holy Monastery of Iviron.

In France, the church of Notre-Dame-des-Miracles at Saint-Maur near Paris also possesses such an icon.

Similarly, the Holy Face of Edessa, in the church of St Bartholomew at Genoa, is said to have been painted by Christ himself (see photo opposite).

The painting of Christ in the Sancta Sanctorum of the Latran, Rome, is said to be the work Saint Luke, but completed by angels. The Veil of Veronica at Saint Peter's in Rome is traditionally considered as an acheiropoieton in some quarters.

The famous *Volto Santo di Lucca* (Holy Face of Lucca), Tuscany, attributed to Nicodemus, who was present at Christ's crucifixion with Joseph of Arimathea, is also said to have been completed by angels (see *Secret Tuscany* in this collection of guides).

In Venice there are two acheiropoietic sculptures: one in the church of Santi Geremia e Lucia and the other in the church of San Marziale, both in Cannaregio.

In the Abruzzi region of Italy there is a *Volto Santo* at the village of Manoppello.

WHEN DID THE JUBILEE YEAR BEGIN TO BE CELEBRATED EVERY 25 YEARS?

The Jubilee tradition comes from the Jewish law according to which a holy year is decreed every 50 years, at the end of seven cycles each of seven years (Leviticus). Slaves recovered their freedom and the land its former owners.

The word "jubilee" is from the Hebrew *Yôbel*, literally a billy goat, and by extension its horns and the horn that was sounded on great occasions.

The first recorded Jubilee took place in 1300 during the reign of Pope Boniface VIII: believing that a visit to the tombs of Saint Paul and Saint Peter would give rise to special indulgences (see following double page) in that year of the 13th centenary of the birth of Christ, the number of pilgrims flocking to Rome dramatically increased. Thus the pope clarified the conditions for obtaining full indulgences (15 visits – 30 for Romans – to the tombs of Saint Peter and Saint Paul), and initiated the tradition of Jubilees and the pilgrimages associated with them.

The flow of pilgrims filled the coffers of the Church and from the mid-15th century a rhythm of one Jubilee every 25 years was established, while the conditions for the granting of indulgences became stricter: in addition to the indispensable confession of sin, pilgrims were required to visit not only the basilicas of Saint Peter and Saint Paul, but also the

Lateran basilica from 1350 and that of Saint Mary Major from 1373.

Since 1750, conditions for the granting of a full indulgence have been visiting all four major or papal basilicas, confession, communion and prayer.

In modern times, the most recent Jubilees were held in 1950, 1983 (extraordinary Jubilee to celebrate the 1,950th anniversary of Christ's Passion) and 2000. In theory the next will take place in 2025.

ONE BRICK OF GOLD AND ONE OF SILVER

According to the door-closing ritual established in 1500, and still followed today, two cardinals place two small bricks, one gold and the other silver, in the wall.

TOOLS FOR OPENING HOLY DOORS

The four major basilicas of Rome (Saint Peter in the Vatican, Saint Mary Major, Saint John Lateran and Saint Paul Outside the Walls) are the only four churches in Christendom to possess a holy door. What is distinctive about them is that they are only opened during Jubilees, i.e. every 25 years, other than on a special Jubilee decreed by the pope. Their opening has symbolised the beginning of the Holy Year (Jubilee) since 24 December 1499, when Pope Alexander VI Borgia inaugurated this rite at Saint Peter's, although the first holy door to be opened was in fact that of the Lateran basilica, by Pope Martin V in 1423.

The opening of the holy doors takes place on Christmas Eve. The door of Saint Peter's is broken down symbolically by the pope in person, who knocks three times with a gold and silver hammer. The doors of the three other churches were opened by the cardinals of each basilica until 1983. On the occasion of the Great Jubilee of 2000, however, the pontiff opened the four doors himself.

Once open, Saint Peter's holy door is walled up again on 6 January of the following year (5 January for the three other basilicas), with the pope blessing the tools used in its reconstruction and symbolically laying the first three stones.

Although since 1975 the holy door has been directly visible from the outside, this was not always the case: from 1500 to 1975 the holy door was walled up from the exterior, and the wall had to be physically knocked down. So the pope used a hammer, examples of which quickly became precious relics and, during reconstruction, a trowel, even though the *sampietrini* (Vatican workmen) obviously took over from him to finish the work.

Some of these relics can still be seen, notably in the treasuries of the basilicas of Saint Peter and Saint Mary Major.

In 1974, debris from the destruction of the wall fell just beside Pope Paul VI and could have injured him, hence changes were made in 1975. Since then, the wall that closed off the door from the outside has been reconstructed inside the basilica and the pope merely has to close the two sections of the door.

INDULGENCES: "AS SOON AS THE MONEY CLINKS IN THE COLLECTION-BOX, THE SOUL FLIES OUT OF PURGATORY."

In Roman Catholic doctrine, sins are erased by the sacrament of penance. But the confessional does not remove the pain of Purgatory, a place from which sinners hope to be liberated as quickly as possible. The length of time spent in Purgatory can be reduced or even written off completely by the granting of indulgences. These can be partial or full, depending on whether they free the penitent partially or totally from the duration of punishment for the sin in question. An indulgence is obtained in exchange for an act of piety (such as pilgrimage, prayer, mortification), carried out to this end in a spirit of repentance. Partial indulgences were traditionally counted in days, months or years. Contrary to what one might think, they do not correspond to an equivalent amount of direct remission from Purgatory, but indicate the remission corresponding to a particular penance. This practice, handed down from Roman law, goes back to the 3rd century, when it was important to bring back into the fold those Christians who had denied their religion because of persecution. "Simony" is a corruption of the practice of indulgence: the faithful made a bargain with the priest through an act of charity, which often took the form of a cash donation... A notorious example dates from 1515: that year, the Dominican friar Johann Tetzel was responsible for the sale of indulgences in the name of the Archbishop of Mainz, Albrecht von Brandenburg, who deducted 50% of the money to cover his household expenses. The hugely cynical motto of the enterprising monk, who beat a drum to attract the crowds, was "As soon as the money clinks in the collection-box, the soul flies out of Purgatory." It was against this background of scandal that Martin Luther intervened on 31 October 1517, the eve of All Saint's Day, posting his Ninety-five Theses denouncing the practice. The dispute over indulgences became one of the main causes of the schism between Protestants and Catholics.

In 1967, Pope Paul VI suppressed the references to a fixed number of days or years, but the indulgence itself, although perhaps less well known today, is still practised: during the millennium Jubilee celebrations, for example, indulgences were granted by Pope John Paul II. Protestants objected in vain. Five centuries may have gone by, but history repeats itself ...

Simony is the term used by Christians to refer to the buying or selling of pardons and other spiritual privileges. The practice owes its name to a certain Simon Magus, who practiced sorcery and wished to buy Saint Peter's ability to work miracles (Acts 8: 9-21), earning him the apostle's condemnation: "May your silver perish with you, because you have thought that the gift of God may be purchased with money!"

SOULS IN PURGATORY

While you can shorten your own stay in Purgatory (see above), it is also possible to alleviate the pain of souls already there, in what is known as the communion of saints.

When a living Christian prays for a soul in Purgatory, that soul sees its time reduced. Equally, a soul in Purgatory can intervene on behalf of a living person...

SIGHTS NEARBY

THE OPTICAL ILLUSION OF VIA PICCOLOMINI

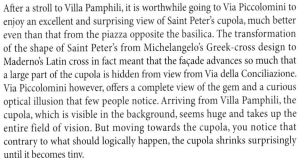

Via Piccolomini • Bus 982

After a stroll to Villa Pamphili, it is worthwhile going to Via Piccolomini to enjoy an excellent and surprising view of Saint Peter's cupola, much better even than that from the piazza opposite the basilica. The transformation of the shape of Saint Peter's from Michelangelo's Greek-cross design to Maderno's Latin cross in fact meant that the façade advances so much that a large part of the cupola is hidden from view from Via della Conciliazione. Via Piccolomini however, offers a complete view of the gem and a curious optical illusion that few people notice. Arriving from Villa Pamphili, the cupola, which is visible in the background, seems huge and takes up the entire field of vision. But moving towards the cupola, you notice that contrary to what should logically happen, the cupola shrinks surprisingly until it becomes tiny.

THE ROMAN NECROPOLIS OF VIA TRIUMPHALIS

• Tours Fridays and Saturdays for groups of 25 maximum
• Reservation required by writing to the special visits office of the Vatican Museums
• E-mail: visitedidattiche.musei@scv.va
• Admission (guide included): €8 per person

In 2003, during construction work on an underground car park in Vatican City, archaeologists made an exceptional discovery: they unearthed a new sector of the vast necropolis that extended along Via Triumphalis, the ancient route linking Rome with Veio. The first part of this route had already been discovered in the 1950s during the construction of another parking lot in the Vatican (incidentally known as the "Necropolis car park").

Although some of the thousands of tourists who descend every day on the Vatican Museums seem to have been aware of the magnificent necropolis of Via Cornelia concealed in the basement of the basilica (where Saint Peter's tomb can be viewed), not many know of this recent discovery, chiefly because it has only been open to the public since 2006.

The digs revealed around forty funerary structures, some of which were decorated with frescoes and stucco or covered with mosaics, as well as over 200 individual tombs on several levels, not to mention tombstones, stelae and innumerable inscriptions, some of which indicated the place of birth and occupation of the deceased.

The tombs, which date back to a period from the reign of Augustus to that of Constantine, are in excellent condition. As they were being unearthed, some, still intact, even contained sarcophagi decorated with bas reliefs, urns, oil lamps and containers for offerings to the dead.

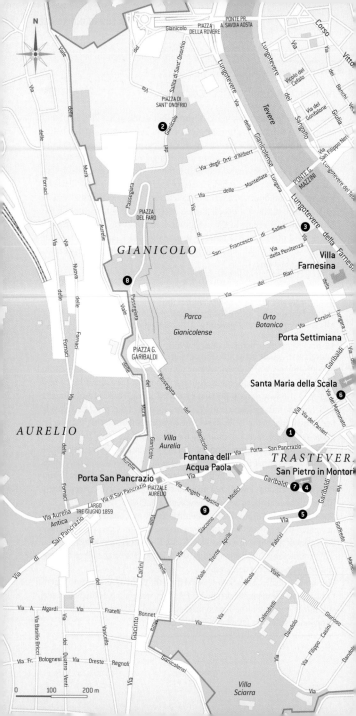

GIANICOLO

BOSCO PARRASIO

❶

32 Via di Porta San Pancrazio
- Bus: 115, 870
- Opening times: contact Accademia dell'Arcadia, 8 Piazza San Agostino
- E-mail: giovannarak@gmail.com
- Tel: 06 4872607

The arcadian grove

Bosco Parrasio, former home of the Accademia dell'Arcadia (Academy of Arcadia - an Italian literary academy), is a beautiful garden attributed to Francesco de Sanctis, who also designed the Spanish Steps of Trinità dei Monti. Antonio Canevari, responsible for carrying out the work, found an ingenious solution to the problem posed by the sloping land, dividing it into three levels, joined by concave and convex flights of steps. On the upper level, there is an oval theatre with three rows of seats and a marble lectern, where poets would read their verses. The *Serbatoio* (literally reservoir or tank) building in the background housed the academy's archives and secretarial office. It was restructured in 1838 by Giovanni Azzurri, giving it a semi-circular façade, on which the academy's laws and the inscription *Deo nato sacrum* are displayed. This Latin inscription is a reminder that the garden is dedicated to the Baby Jesus. On the middle level a grotto was constructed, and on the lower level a large marble

edicola (shrine) with an inscription dating from 1726 commemorates the donation from the King of Portugal that made the project possible. This place knew a period of glory thanks to the presence of great men among its academicians, such as the poet Pietro Metastasio and the philosopher Giambattista Vico. At the end of the 18th century, with the decline of the Arcadians, it was abandoned, but reopened in 1839, after restoration work. Bosco Parrasio still belongs to the academy.

The name *Parrasio* comes from an area in southern Arcadia, Parrasia.

THE *ACCADEMIA DELL'ARCADIA*

In 1690 a group of Italian intellectuals who had been part of Queen Christina of Sweden's circle, concerned about the neglected state of literature, founded the Accademia dell'Arcadia in homage to *Arcadia* (1504), a pastoral romance by Jacopo Sannazaro, and to the Greek region of Arcadia, with the objective of returning to the purity of the classical texts as a reaction against Baroque "bad taste". The president took the name of Great Keeper, in reference to the role of shepherd, the members became known as *pastorelli* and *pastorelle* (young male and female shepherds) and Baby Jesus, born among shepherds, was declared protector of the academy. For years the Arcadians would meet in one garden or another, until, in 1726, they founded their permanent headquarters at the foot of Janiculum Hill, alongside the gardens of Palazzo Corsini, former residence of Queen Christina, acquired through the beneficence of John V, King of Portugal, who donated 4,000 escudos to the institution.

ARCADIA: AN ESOTERIC TASTE OF PARADISE?

Arcadia is a mountainous region of Greece's central and eastern Peloponnese.

In antiquity it was considered a primitive and idyllic place where shepherds lived in harmony with nature. In this respect it symbolised a golden age echoed by numerous literary and artistic works: Virgil's *Bucolics* or Ovid's *Fasti* ("Calendar"), for example.

Rediscovered during the Renaissance and 17th century, Arcadia again came to signify the ideal, although for many scholars it represented much more.

The ancient region was celebrated in the 17th century by the French painter Poussin and his canvas *Les Bergers d'Arcadie* ("The Arcadian Shepherds"), now in the Louvre in Paris, in which many see a hidden esoteric message. See also page 28 (Poussin's tomb).

The Alpheus River winds its way through Arcadia and is said to run underground to the sea and resurface in Sicily, where its waters mingle with the fountain of Arethusa.

Alpheus was a sacred river-god, the mythological son of the Titan Oceanus and his sister Tethys, whose underground streams symbolised the hidden traditions of esoteric knowledge.

So this knowledge, which is transmitted to certain artists, was found in the work of Leonardo da Vinci, Botticelli and Poussin, among others.

The name Arcadia comes from Arcas, itself from the ancient Greek *arktos*, meaning "bear". In Greek mythology, Arcas, king of Arcadia, was the son of Zeus and the nymph Callisto. The legend goes that Callisto had offended the goddess Artemis, the huntress, who changed her into a bear during a hunt. Callisto, killed in the chase, was placed among the stars by Zeus and became the *Ursa Major* (Great Bear) constellation, while her son Arcas was transformed into *Ursa Minor* on his death.

THE CROSS OF THE ORDER OF THE HOLY SEPULCHRE OF JERUSALEM

The insignia of the order is the red Jerusalem cross or cross potent (with crossbars), surrounded by four smaller crosses. These five crosses now serve as a reminder of the five wounds of Christ on the Cross, even though they originally signified that the Word of Christ had spread in four directions around the world.

The symbolism is also of resurrection.

The colour red, representing life, strength and blood, was chosen to commemorate the wounds inflicted on Christ.

In the East, the cross is golden, symbolising the immense value of Christ's Passion.

SIGHTS NEARBY

MONASTERY OF SANT'ONOFRIO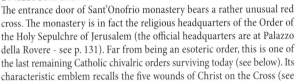
2 Piazza Sant'Onofrio

The entrance door of Sant'Onofrio monastery bears a rather unusual red cross. The monastery is in fact the religious headquarters of the Order of the Holy Sepulchre of Jerusalem (the official headquarters are at Palazzo della Rovere - see p. 131). Far from being an esoteric order, this is one of the last remaining Catholic chivalric orders surviving today (see below). Its characteristic emblem recalls the five wounds of Christ on the Cross (see opposite page).

THE BELFRY OF SAN GIACOMO ALLA LUNGARA
12 Lungotevere della Farnesina

Walking along Via della Lungara towards Porta Settimiana, on the corner with Salita del Buon Pastore, the small church of San Giacomo rises in front of you, with a convent annexed to it. The church dates back to the 9th century and it has a small and beautiful belfry, decorated with marble medallions, enclosed by rows of zigzagging brick. It is now hemmed in between later buildings, and is only visible from Lungotevere. The belfry has the peculiarity of being the only remaining Romanesque belfry in Rome with one opening. It was built in the 13th century, when Pope Innocent IV gave the church to the Sylvestrine nuns. Parts of the masonry in bare brick possibly belonged to an older, already existing tower.

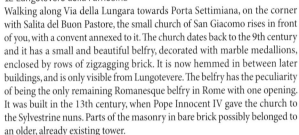

ORDER OF THE HOLY SEPULCHRE OF JERUSALEM

The Order of the Holy Sepulchre of Jerusalem is a military and religious chivalric order of knighthood thought to have been founded by Duke Godfrey of Bouillon, victor of the First Crusade in 1099 at Jerusalem, or even, according to other sources, by Charlemagne (in 808). With its headquarters in Rome at Sant'Onofrio monastery on Janiculum Hill, the order has thirty-five branches around the world.

There are some 18,000 Knights and Ladies of the Holy Sepulchre, whose principal aim is to encourage and propagate their faith in the Holy Land, under the authority of the pope.

The order owes its name to the Holy Cross of Jerusalem, the sanctuary built around the supposed site of Christ's crucifixion and the place where he is thought to have been buried and resurrected.

Today the order runs forty-four Catholic schools in and around Jerusalem, bringing together some 15,000 pupils, both Christian and Muslim.

In France, the order is the guardian of the holy relic of Christ's crown of thorns (see *Secret Paris* in this series of guides).

SIGHTS NEARBY

JANICULUM HILL: THE TRUE LOCATION OF SAINT PETER'S CRUCIFIXION?

Tempietto de Bramante - Piazza San Pietro in Montorio, 2
• Opening times: Opening times: April to September, 9:30am-12:30pm
and 4pm-6pm (2pm-4pm from October to March), except Mondays

According to one tradition, different of course from the official version which maintains that these events took place on the hill of the Vatican, the apostle Saint Peter may actually have been crucified on the hill called Janiculum, at the site where the Tempietto de Bramante now stands. Janiculum was indeed used back in those times as a site for the crucifixion of criminals and slaves. Saint Peter, who had put an end to the magical practices of Simon Magus (see page 215), was responsible for the latter's death. Consequently considered by some to be an assassin, he is said to have been crucified at the exact spot of the well behind the Bramante monument. The bas-reliefs featured here recall that Saint Peter supposedly asked to be crucified head down, as he felt himself unworthy of being crucified in a manner similar to Christ.

THE VIA GARIBALDI LATRINES

Via G. Garibaldi (near Piazza San Pietro in Montorio)
• Visits on request, by telephoning the Cultural Heritage department of the Municipality of Rome (*Sovraintendenza Comunale ai Beni Culturali*) at 06 0608, alternatively through cultural associations such as *Roma Sotterranea* (www.romasotterranea.it).

In 1963, the collapse of a retaining wall next to the church of San Pietro in Montorio revealed an unexpected public facility: Roman latrines dating from the end of the 2nd century AD. You can reach them by pushing your way through the undergrowth to find a little door. Inside, the walls are decorated with frescoes of geometric patterns in green and red. The illustrations include plant motifs and an ibex. These artworks are nevertheless of rather less interest than the vast quantity of later graffiti representing animals, obscene symbols and human figures, as well as Latin or Greek examples of lavatory humour. All these spontaneous expressions are a clear sign that subversive graffiti is nothing new. On the other hand, there is no trace of any stone lavatory seats, so they were probably made from wood. Below, a canal has been dug to evacuate waste to the sewers. Under the tiles another canal can be glimpsed, smaller than the first, where clean water probably ran for use in sponging down the latrines. The black and white tiles with geometric motifs have only been preserved on a small portion of the floor.

BORROMINI'S STAIRCASE

Crypt of the monastery of Santa Maria dei Sette Dolori
Hotel Donna Camilla Savelli - Via Garibaldi, 27 • Tel.: 06 588861

At the foot of Janiculum Hill, there is also the monastery of Santa Maria dei Sette Dolori with its adjoining church, whose façade has never been completed due to lack of funds. The crypt of the monastery, now transformed into an elegant hotel, conceals solid ancient and medieval walls which form the foundations of the church. Here, Borromini in his genius did not alter the existing structures, but simply added a grand staircase, opening another dimension for viewing the walls in rough masonry, the beaten earth floor and a row of beams with barrels resting on them. In the future, the crypt will probably be opened to the public as plans are afoot to convert this space, without making any major changes, for wine tastings.

MINISTERO PER I BENI CULTURALI E AMBIENTALI

SOPRINTENDENZA PER I BENI AMBIENTALI ED ARCHITETTONICI DI ROMA

PROIETTILE DI CANNONE DA 140
DELL'ARTIGLIERIA FRANCESE
~ MEMORIA BELLICA
DEI BOMBARDAMENTI
DEL GIUGNO 1849~
QUI' TROVATO E RIPOSTO
IN RICORDO
DELL'EROICA RESISTENZA DELLA REPUBBLICA ROMANA
E DEI GRAVI DANNI ALLORA SOFFERTI
DA QUESTA INSIGNE CAPPELLA
~ORA NUOVAMENTE RESTAURATA~
OPERA DI CARLO MADERNO

A. D. MDCCCCXCV

SAN PIETRO IN MONTORIO'S CANNON BALL ❼

Outside wall of the church of San Pietro in Montorio
Via Garibaldi

I f you look to the left on the façade of the church of San Pietro in Montorio, you will see a strange plaque with a sphere attached to it. Step closer to read the inscription and you will discover a French artillery cannon ball found at this very spot. It commemorates the 1849 battles during which the independent republic of Rome put up a heroic defence.

An unusual souvenir of the fighting on Janiculum Hill in 1849

1849 was a decisive year for the Risorgimento, the ideological and political movement behind Italian unification. In Rome, papal rule foundered in the face of popular pro-democracy uprisings, and the pope was obliged to flee the city. The republic was proclaimed on 9 February. The conservative European regimes offered help to restore temporal power while Garibaldi and his followers disembarked at Rome to defend the new republic. He was entrusted with the defence of Janiculum Hill, the point most exposed to the French army offensive.

GARIBALDI: SAVIOUR OF TASSO'S BELL

It was in 1595 that the smallest bell of the church of Sant'Onofrio al Gianicolo had come to be known as "Tasso's bell". On 25 April of that year, its melancholy peals accompanied the death throes and announced the end – at the age of only 51 – of the celebrated poet who was being cared for in the neighbouring convent.

In spring 1849, this bell was almost destroyed during the rioting that gripped the capital. The order had gone out to confiscate all church bells to make cannons, and as it was not far from the fighting Sant'Onofrio was one of the first churches to be requisitioned by the military.

The story goes that the Father Superior vainly begged the officer in charge to take whatever he liked except the little bell, but he would not be moved, until Garibaldi arrived in the nick of time. As a last resort, the priest appealed directly to the general.

Moved by his supplications, or perhaps by the sad early death of a great poet, Garibaldi ordered that Tasso's bell be spared.

Thus it can still be seen today, as well as the tomb and the convent cell where the unfortunate author of the immortal *Gerusalemme liberata* died.

VILLA LANTE

10 Passeggiata del Gianicolo
• Tel: 06 68801674
• E-mail: : info@irfrome.org
• Bus: 115, 870
• Visits on request from Monday to Friday, 9am - 12pm
Amici di Villa Lante al Gianicolo association: €25 annual membership
includes invitations to conferences, concerts and exhibitions

An unbeatable view

Villa Lante on Janiculum Hill, one of the best-preserved 16th-century Roman villas, is a priceless example of the work of Raphael's school in Rome. It offers an exceptional view, perhaps the most beautiful in the city.

The villa, with its three arches, four antique columns in purple-veined Phrygian marble and a stucco-decorated vault, is nevertheless little known, as it is not visible from the street.

Its construction dates back to when Baldassare Turini, Pope Leo X's datarius (papal official), bought some 2 hectares of land on Janiculum Hill, covered in vineyards and gardens at the time, as a summer residence and to welcome other officials and the literati.

Giulio Romano, Raphael's favourite student, was the architect, and other artists from the school carried out the pictorial decoration. The original decoration of the salon, with its imitation marble and precious stones, was discovered and restored in the 1970s on part of the walls, whereas elsewhere the neoclassical work by the renowned architect Valadier was retained. The famous graffiti "A dì 6 de maggio 1527 fo la presa di Roma", representing the sacking of Rome, is still visible in the salon.

In 1551 the property went to the Lante family, who lived in a palazzo in Piazza Sant'Eustachio. The size of the villa's garden was reduced in 1640, when Pope Urban VIII decided to build the Janiculum defensive wall and in exchange gave the Lante family the villa in Bagnaia, close to Viterbo, with its spectacular park filled with fountains.

At the beginning of the 19th century, the Lante family sold part of their property, including the villa, which passed to Prince Camillo Borghese, husband of Napoleon's sister Pauline, who in turn sold it a few years later to the order of nuns of the Sacred Heart of Jesus. The frescoes in the salon, which were not part of the sale, were removed from the ceiling and now can be found in Palazzo Zuccari. At the end of the 19th century, the nuns rented the villa to the German archaeologist Wolfgang Helbig and his wife, the Russian princess Nadine Schahawskoy, who converted it into a much-frequented cultural centre.

AMERICAN ACADEMY IN ROME ❾

5 Via Angelo Masina
• Tel.: 06 58461
• info@aarome.org
• Open to the public for exhibitions, concerts, lectures and more
• Programme available at www.aarome.org

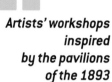

Artists' workshops inspired by the pavilions of the 1893 Chicago World's Fair

The American Academy, even more discreet than other similar Roman institutions, accepts some thirty artists and researchers per year, as well as around forty short-stay students.

The project to set up an American Academy in Rome emerged following the Chicago Columbian Exposition of 1893 and was based on the idea of a group led by two architects: Charles Follen McKim, who designed some of the buildings of the University of Colombia (1893) and the Pierpont Morgan Library (1903) in New York; and Daniel Burnham, responsible for the Flatiron Building in New York (1902).

These men attached great significance to European classical culture, and would convince the biggest New York financiers of the time (J.P. Morgan, John D. Rockefeller and Henry Clay Frick) to make substantial donations to establish the American Academy in Rome in 1894.

Today, the artists' workshops in front of the outer façade are reminiscent of the pavilions of the 1893 Expo, while the academy's main building, designed by McKim, Mead and White, was inspired by Renaissance villas with a *piano nobile* (main floor) and a courtyard ornamented with the remains of antique sculptures.

The beautiful Villa Aurelia was built for Cardinal Girolamo Farnese in 1650. In 1849, Garibaldi set up his headquarters there to defend the Roman Republic against the French armies, whose artillery almost destroyed the villa and its gardens in their victorious battle. After major restoration work, the villa was bequeathed to the American Academy in 1909. Conferences and concerts are regularly held there.

In the gardens, the Casa Rustica stands on the site of the 16th-century casino of Cardinal Malvasia. On 14 April 1611, the Academia dei Lincei held a grand reception there in honour of Galileo, whose guests could view the heavens through the telescope he had invented. The casino was demolished in 1849 and replaced by the Casa Rustica, which houses maps produced by NASA representing the sky on 14 April 1611. The building was used as a tavern until the 1920s (the inscription "VINO" can still be seen), when it was bought by the Academy.

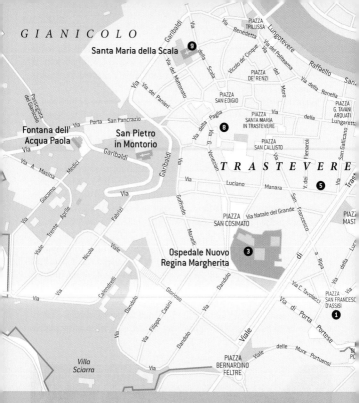

TRASTEVERE

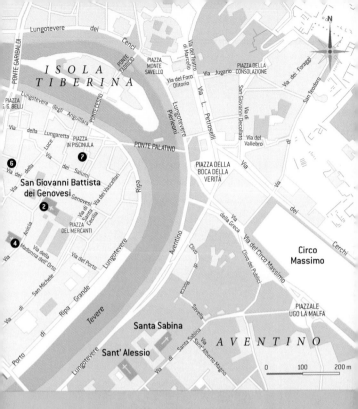

THE MECHANISM OF THE RELIQUARY OF SAINT FRANCIS' CELL

❶

San Francesco d'Assisi a Ripa Grande
Piazza San Francesco d'Assisi
• Tel.: 06 5819020
• Open 9am-12pm and 4:30pm-7:30pm

> **Relics hidden in a precious artefact**

Saint Francis of Assisi and his disciples were lodged in a cell annexed to this church, which belonged to Benedictine monks before it was named San Francesco d'Assisi a Ripa Grande, Pope Gregory IX having asked the monks in 1229 to hand over their church and the adjacent hospice to the Order of Friars Minor (the Franciscans).

It is not widely known that this cell, later converted into a chapel, holds a curious Baroque masterpiece: an amazing altar was carved from the roots of a walnut tree between 1698 and 1708 by the Franciscan brother Bernardino da Jesi, and later embellished with traditional paintings.

In the middle of the wood panelling is a magnificent 13th-century altarpiece featuring a portrait of Saint Francis attributed to the school of Margheritone d'Arezzo. The altarpiece is flanked by two 14th-century paintings depicting Saint Anthony of Padua and Saint Louis of Toulouse, while the side panels feature the Virgin and the Angel of the Annunciation, late 17th-century works by an artist of the school of Carlo Maratta. It was Cardinal Ranuccio Pallavicini who commissioned this rare artefact for the church, to which he also bequeathed his impressive collection of relics. The altarpiece in fact incorporates an ingenious mechanism: the

relics are kept inside the altar, in precious silver coffers. When the mechanism is activated, all the visible parts pivot to reveal the treasures inside, thus transforming the altar into a sumptuous reliquary.

Next to the altar, in a niche closed by a grille, a stone on which Saint Francis is said to have laid his head has also been preserved.

THE CLOISTER OF SAN GIOVANNI DEI GENOVESI

12 Via Anicia
• Open Tuesdays and Thursdays, 2pm-4pm in winter and 3pm-5pm in summer

> *A little-known 15th-century marvel*

Among the maze of buildings in the Trastevere district is the headquarters of the brotherhood of Saint John the Baptist, where one of the most beautiful cloisters in Rome is hidden from the street. Access is via the church through a little door in the left-hand wall.

You will find yourself in a haven of peace and silence, immediately entranced by the beauty of the ground-floor archways buttressed onto octagonal columns and the architraves of the upper storey, as well as the contrast between their shade and the luxuriant green plants bathed in sunshine. In the centre of the garden stands a 14th-century travertine well, set off by two antique columns in Ionic style.

Fragments of antique marble are scattered here and there beneath the arcades. The church and most of the buildings were given so many facelifts between the 15th and 19th centuries that they have lost their original appearance, with the exception of the old hospice and the cloister, built in 1481 and attributed to Baccio Pontelli, designer of the Sistine Chapel.

An inscription on a funerary stele explains that inside the cloister there used to be a compound, demolished at the end of the 18th century, while another inscription on a column, in Latin this time, says that in this cloister the very first palm tree to be imported to Rome was planted by a friar from Savona in the late 16th century.

The cycle of frescoes attributed to Guido Signorini and Gerolamo Margotti date from the beginning of the 17th century, however. They were discovered in the 1970s under a thick coat of lime-washed plaster during the restoration of the site.

The brotherhood was founded in 1533, although the church dedicated to Saint John the Baptist (patron saint of the city of Genoa) and its hospice (founded by Pope Sixtus IV and paid for by the Genoese ambassador to help sailors) already existed.

WHY IS JOHN THE BAPTIST THE PATRON SAINT OF GENOA?

Around the year 1100, on the way back to Genoa from the Crusades, Genoese sailors stopped off along the coast of Lycia (now south-western Turkey) and found the ashes of Saint John the Baptist in a convent, not far from the town of Myra (modern Demre). Following this episode, the town adopted the saint as its patron.

THE CLOISTERS OF THE NUOVO REGINA MARGHERITA HOSPITAL

Piazza San Cosimato
• Tram 8

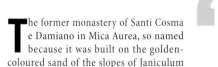

*Hidden
cloisters*

The former monastery of Santi Cosma e Damiano in Mica Aurea, so named because it was built on the golden-coloured sand of the slopes of Janiculum Hill, later became known as San Cosimato. Today, it is part of the Nuovo Regina Margherita hospital complex, opened in 1970.

Apart from hospital staff, patients and their families, and passers-by, few people know that the hospital grounds contain two spectacular cloisters. The first is medieval, dating back to the beginning of the 12th century, and the other Renaissance, built during restoration work commissioned by Pope Sixtus IV.

The first cloister, which was one of the biggest in medieval Rome, is the most impressive. With arcades on all four sides, small twin columns supporting the narrow brick arches, the cloister is filled with fragments of ancient inscriptions. Columns and sarcophagi are scattered over the lawn and among the trees in the garden.

A few steps lead up to the second cloister. There are arcades on all four sides with small twin columns supporting the narrow brick arches, and the cloister is filled with fragments of ancient inscriptions.

San Cosimato, with its complex architectural history divided between two medieval periods and the Renaissance, was for centuries one of the richest monasteries in Rome.

The monastery, founded in the first half of the 10th century by Benedictine monks, was not completed until the 13th century. The Franciscan Order of Poor Clare nuns took over the convent in 1234 and had it enlarged. This was followed by work carried out under Pope Sixtus IV for the 1475 Jubilee, during which a new church, a belfry and the second cloister were constructed.

After the unification of Italy and the introduction of legislation suppressing religious corporations, the Italian state ceded San Cosimato convent to the City of Rome. It was granted to a charitable organisation and then converted into a hospice.

THE FORTY-HOUR DEVICE

Church of Santa Maria dell'Orto
10 Via Anicia
• Tram 8, station Trastevere/Piazza Mastai
• Open daily, 9am-12pm
• Device only on view during the 50 days following Easter

O n the main altar of the church of Santa Maria dell'Orto, designed by Giacomo della Porta, the superb "forty-hour device", much more meaningful than just a mechanism, is an amazing structure that holds 213 candles. Built by Luigi Clementi in 1848, it is based on a medieval Easter tradition in which a consecrated wafer was placed in a symbolic tomb during the forty hours that Jesus would have spent in the tomb between Good Friday (his death) and Easter Sunday (his resurrection).

Forty hours, the time that Jesus spent in the tomb

In the 16th century this ritual was replaced by periods of forty hours of continuous prayer. The faithful went from church to church to pray and the altars were often adorned with a temporary structure (known as the *apparato*) housing the communion host.

At the end of the 16th century, in order to distract people from the temptations of carnival festivals, the Roman clerics established the custom of celebrating the forty hours over nine days in February, in the churches of San Lorenzo in Damaso and the Gesù, which led Pietro da Cortona to construct a superb forty-hour device in 1632 for San Lorenzo in Damaso. Most of the time, these devices were built using materials that were easy to work with, like the wooden structures on which stucco or papier mâché decorations could be added. The one in Santa Maria dell'Orto is very finely worked, so well that it has evolved from a temporary to a permanent structure, the last of its kind to survive in Rome.

It is still used today during the Mass of the Last Supper on Holy (Maundy) Thursday: all the candles of the main altar are lit at the same time. On this occasion the church remains open until midnight so that the faithful can gather around this spectacle, as leaving the candles lit for forty hours is no longer feasible for technical reasons.

ANATOMY THEATRE OF SAN GALLICANO HOSPITAL

Sede Storica Istituto San Gallicano
25 Via San Gallicano, Trastevere
• Open Saturdays, 10am-4pm

> *A room for dissecting corpses*

Within the constantly busy precincts of the Santa Maria e San Gallicano hospital can be found its former anatomy theatre. Here, in this room decorated with stucco bas-reliefs, dissections of human bodies used to be carried out. On the floor, below the light flooding from the pierced vault, a large marble slab marks the location of the table on which the corpses lay. The room is now headquarters to the institute's scientific management.

Pope Leo XII had this anatomy theatre built in 1826 to celebrate the centenary of the Institute of Santa Maria and San Gallicano. The architect Giacomo Palazzi was commissioned to design this oval room at the centre of which opens a round vault surrounded by allegories of medicine. Around the sides, stucco medallions depict eighteen illustrious Roman doctors, from Celsus, known as the Latin Hippocrates (1st century AD) to the great anatomist Gabriele Fallopio (1523-1562) who described certain essential aspects of the reproductive and auditory systems, and Lancisi (1654-1720) who established the correlation between mosquitoes and malaria.

The main beauty of this room lies in the stucco bas-reliefs sculpted by Ignazio del Sarti, representing the legend of Asclepius as recounted in Ovid's *Metamorphoses* (see below).

WAS ASCLEPIUS, GOD OF MEDICINE, BEHIND THE CREATION OF TIBER ISLAND?

According to Ovid's account in *Metamorphoses*, when a great plague decimated the population of Rome, the Romans went to consult the oracle at Delphi. The prophetess replied that they needed the help of her son, the god of medicine, rather than Apollo. So the Roman Senate sent a delegation to fetch Asclepius by ship from Epidaurus. He told them that he would appear as a serpent and that they would need to recognise him in this form. The Romans prayed to the god and a great serpent appeared, which they allowed on board. The serpent dispelled the perils of the voyage and the ship sailed safely back up the Tiber. On arriving at Rome, the serpent wrapped itself around the trunk of a tree. At this very spot the river divided into two channels, creating an island. The serpent then slithered down from the tree and healed Rome's citizens.

There are also well-preserved anatomical theatres in London, Barcelona, Pistoia (Tuscany), Padua and Bologna. See *Secret London – an unusual guide*, *Secret Tuscany*, and *Secret Barcelona* from the same publisher.

THE *EXCUBITORIUM*

Via della Settima Coorte
Tram: 3, 8
• Visits on request, by telephoning the Cultural Heritage department of
the Municipality of Rome (*Sovraintendenza Comunale ai Beni Culturali*)
at 06 0608, alternatively through cultural associations such as *Roma
Sotterranea* (www.romasotterranea.it)

Firemen
from ancient
Rome

During excavation work in the mid-19th
century, some rooms were discovered
from the Roman period about 8 metres
underneath the current street level. The
building was identified as housing a detachment from the seventh cohort of
the city's guards, or firemen, thanks to the large amount of graffiti present on
the walls. The guard corps was composed of seven cohorts, each with 1,000
to 1,200 men. Each cohort had to protect two of the fourteen districts into
which the city was subdivided, and had their barracks in one district and a
detachment (*excubitorium*) in the other.

Unfortunately, the area was abandoned after the excavation work, with
serious consequences for the preservation of the structure and the graffiti of
the ancient firemen. A splendid floor mosaic was also destroyed during the
Second World War. Only a century later was the monument finally roofed over,
while maintenance and restoration work was finished twenty years later.

It seems that these firemen's quarters were installed within a private
residence towards the end of the 2nd century AD. By going down a modern
staircase, you enter a large hall where there is a peculiar hexagonal basin with
concave sides. On the far wall there is a door leading into a *lararium* (chapel)
dedicated to the protector of the guards, *genio excubitori,* in which only the
remains of paintings on the walls of the *edicola* (wall shrine) and on the lintel
are preserved. In other rooms, pieces of terracotta floors have been found with
bricks in an *opus spicatum* or herringbone design as well as a buried *dolium*
(large ceramic jar) in which wine, oil and grain were usually kept.

In the drawings and photographs that document the room's large black
and white floor mosaic that is now gone, two Tritons are visible, one holding a
lighted torch and the other an extinguished torch.

Of all these important remainrelics that had survived until the time of the
excavations, unfortunately hardly anything remains, except for the fresco with
a cherub and seahorses on a door lintel. The most serious loss is that of almost
one hundred pieces of the firemen's graffiti, which fortunately were transcribed
after their discovery. This unique evidence regarding the organisation of the
firemen and their life in these quarters was written on the plastered walls
between AD 215 and AD 245 by the same firemen. The graffiti included
greetings to the emperors, expressed their fatigue and their thanks to the gods
and the *genio excubitori*, and mentioned the name and number of the cohort
and the names and ranks of the guards.

THE CHURCH BELL OF SAN BENEDETTO IN PISCINULA ❼

40 Piazza Piscinula
• Tram: 8
• Open 7:30am-12pm and 5pm-7pm

The smallest bell in Rome

San Benedetto in Piscinula is a small and beautiful 18th-century church. Known as "San Benedettino" by Trastevere residents, it was built on the ruins of the Domus Aniciorum - the house of the Anicii, an old Roman family to which Saint Benedict is said to have belonged, and whose cell is annexed to the church.

Besides the saint's cell, the charming little Romanesque belfry is the real curiosity of this church. Its bell, 45 cm in diameter, is said to be the smallest

and oldest in Rome. The inscription "1069" engraved in the bronze, indicating the year it was made, has survived centuries of wear and is still legible.

The inside of the church is very irregular and, as is often the case in Rome, contains a hotchpotch of works dating back to different periods. The columns go back to the Roman period, and the floor tiles to medieval times. The remains of frescoes depicting scenes from the Old Testament on the right wall, with the Last Judgement opposite, are from the 12th century.

NEARBY

THE FORGOTTEN MOSAICS OF SANTA MARIA IN TRASTEVERE CHURCH ❽

Piazza Santa Maria in Trastevere
• Tel: 06 5814802
• Tram: 8
• Open 7:30am-1pm and 4pm-7pm
• Vestry: open on request

Santa Maria in Trastevere is one of the most beautiful basilicas in Rome, with its 12th-century bell tower (one of the tallest in the city), its Roman columns salvaged from other monuments, and its precious mosaics.

Almost all Romans have admired the extraordinary medieval mosaic featuring the enthroned Virgin and Child at least once.

However, few people know that the oldest mosaics, dating back to the 1st century AD, are the two smallest and most discreet. These magnificent mosaics are set into the walls to the right of the sacristy vestry, and they depict water birds and fishing scenes.

If the vestry is closed, you only need to ask to have it opened.

The exterior mosaics of the church curve inwards to prevent rain damage.

SANDOLA.OMNIA

RAD. CHIN

MIRR. ELECT

CHIN. PITAIA

THE OLD PHARMACY OF SANTA MARIA DELLA SCALA ❾

Piazza Santa Maria della Scala
• Tram: 8
• Opening times: for group visits (only in Italian) contact Father Gaetano
at 06 8414209

A 16th-century pharmacy

The Farmacia di Santa Maria della Scala, which was opened by Carmelites who arrived in Rome in the late 16th century, became famous among convent pharmacies thanks to the various specialities invented there to fight the plague and other serious diseases. The pharmacy managed to keep a free dispensary open to the public until the 1950s and stayed open until 1978.

The upper floor of this old pharmacy has been preserved, above a more modern working establishment, virtually intact, as it was in the 18th century, and offers visitors a unique experience.

One of the monks working in the pharmacy, Brother Basil, became so well-known for his herbal remedies and especially for his famous Acqua Antipestilenziale (Anti-Plague Water), which cured various types of ailments, that kings, cardinals and popes consulted him. In 1726 he began

to teach chemistry, botany and pharmacy to his disciples. The eulogistic inscriptions on two paintings featuring this well-loved monk, who died in 1804 after almost sixty years of professional activity, sum up his life. His famous essays have been carefully preserved as precious artefacts.

Ghezzi's 18th-century painting, which is kept in the vestry, perfectly conveys the idea of the beauty and importance of the pharmacy at the time. It features Brother Basil teaching his disciples, surrounded by stills and mortars, shelves overflowing with heavy tomes, and cupboards with jars filled with salts and herbs.

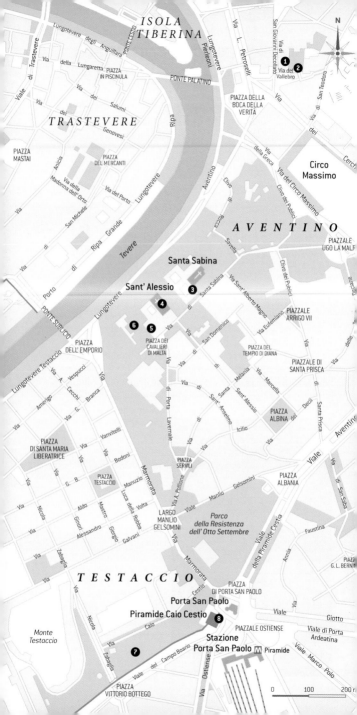

AVENTINO - TESTACCIO

THE FIGURES MISSING FROM THE ARCH ❶
OF THE MONEYCHANGERS

Arco degli Argentarii
Via del Velabro

> *Fratricide between the sons of Septimius Severus*

Just beside the ancient church of San Giorgio al Velabro stands an arch known as the Arco degli Argentarii (Arch of the Moneychangers), for it was the moneychangers of Rome who together with the meat merchants dedicated this monumental gateway to the emperor Septimius Severus.

The arch was not simply ornamental but probably served as one of the main points of access to the Forum Boarium, the ancient cattle market. Rich decoration with plant motifs covers almost the entire surface of the pillars and architrave. You can still read the original inscription, with the dedication dating from AD 204 to Septimius Severus, his wife Julia Domna and his son Bassianus, better known as Caracalla. The nickname came from a floor-length cloak that he had made fashionable. The inner faces of the pillars show Caracalla carrying out a religious sacrifice, on the left, and the imperial family, on the right.

If you look more closely you will see among these images empty spaces where other figures have been deliberately obliterated.

After the death of Septimius Severus and according to his wishes, his two sons Caracalla and Geta governed together for almost a year, until Geta was assassinated by his brother, in their mother's arms, according to Aelius Spartianus's account in his *History of Augustus*. Caracalla accused Geta of attempting to poison him and the senate was obliged to believe this story, declaring Geta henceforth a public enemy and sentencing him to *damnatio memoriae*, a sanction that meant his image would be destroyed and his name deleted from all inscriptions.

This enabled Caracalla to erase the name and portrait of his murdered brother, who had certainly been shown alongside his parents, as well as those of his wife Plautilla and his father-in-law, the praetorian prefect Plautianus (commander of the imperial guard).

SIGHTS NEARBY

THE HOLES IN THE ARCH OF THE MONEYCHANGERS ❷
Another notable feature of the back of the arch is a number of holes, drilled in the Middle Ages. They were made by fortune-seekers who believed the story that a great treasure was hidden inside.

THE ORANGE TREE OF SANTA SABINA CLOISTER

③

Basilique de Santa Sabina
Piazza Pietro d'Illiria, 1
• Open 6:30am-1pm and 3:30pm-7pm

> *The legend of Saint Dominic's orange tree*

Santa Sabina basilica, on the Aventine Hill, dates from the 5th century. It is one of the oldest churches in Rome, although it has frequently undergone major conversions since it was built. In the atrium, by a small oval window opening onto the courtyard of the neighbouring convent, an orange tree can be glimpsed growing in the very spot where, according to Dominican traditions, Saint Dominic planted it around 1220.

A number of anecdotes concerning this orange tree, more or less apocryphal, have endured down the ages. One notable claim is that Saint Dominic brought it back from Spain and planted it at the north-west corner of the former four-arched portico (no longer standing) where he liked to sleep. Until then, oranges had never been known to grow in Italy.

For centuries, this tree was described as miraculous, a new plant perennially springing from the dessicated trunk. Saint Francis de Sales (1567-1622) mentioned it in a letter to Saint Jane Frances de Chantal, in which he demonstrated how the tree had become a focus of the cult of Saint Dominic.

Its oranges are said to have been used to make garlands and mementoes for popes and cardinals. And the story goes that the preserved oranges that Catherine of Sienna offered to Urban VI in 1379 came from this miraculous tree.

In 1936, the ground was levelled where the tree grew. During the work, a coin dating from the 14th century was found among its roots.

NAPOLEON ON A 5TH-CENTURY DOOR!

Carved in the 5th century AD, the famous wooden panels covering the church door depict scenes from the Old and New Testaments. Curiously enough, a portrait of Napoleon can be seen there, shown as the pharaoh pursuing the Jews at the crossing of the Red Sea.

In fact, in the first half of the 19th century, a sculptor restoring the door had taken it upon himself to depict Napoleon as a persecutor of God's chosen people.

The reality was somewhat different, however, concerning Napoleon and the Jews: he was the first European monarch to liberate them from their ghettos, such as the one in Venice, and to grant them certain rights.

THE HIDING PLACE OF SAINT ALEXIUS

Church of Santi Boniface e Alessio
Piazza Sant'Alessio 23
• Open 8:30am-12:30pm and 3:30pm-6:30pm

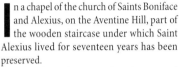

The saint who lived under the stairs

I n a chapel of the church of Saints Boniface and Alexius, on the Aventine Hill, part of the wooden staircase under which Saint Alexius lived for seventeen years has been preserved.

Before the 10th century, there is no record of Saint Alexius in the West, but from then on his celebrity became such that he inspired frescoes (a fine example of which is conserved in the Lower Basilica of San Clemente), poems and pieces of music which have fascinating histories.

Alexius was miraculously born to noble but barren parents in Rome. Although raised in the lap of luxury, he fled to Odessa in the East, where he lived on charity for several years as an ascetic. When his reputation for sanctity grew to be a burden, Alexius decided to leave and sail to Tarsa, but the direction of the wind, or perhaps destiny, took him instead to Ostia. He headed for Rome and presented himself at his father's house. His father welcomed him without recognising him; thinking that he was a beggar, he offered shelter beneath the staircase. Alexius lived there for seventeen years and wrote his life story on a roll of paper. Only when he died did his family discover his true identity, revealed in the scroll that he still clutched in his hand.

The church dates back to the 4th century, when Pope Honorius III ordered the reconstruction of a building dedicated to Saint Boniface already erected on the Aventine. In 1217, it was also dedicated to Saint Alexius.

The plan of the church, which owes its current appearance to restorations of the 16th, 17th and 19th centuries, is a replica of the Roman building with three naves, where you can still see the belltower and crypt (which has a fresco painted between the 13th and 14th centuries, the only example of its kind in Rome) from whence came the fragment of staircase preserved in the chapel of Sant'Alessio.

Antonio Bergondi, apprentice sculptor to Bernini, executed a marble statue for this chapel, representing the saint as a pilgrim on his deathbed.

In the church there is also a well that, it is said, formerly stood within the house of Alexius' father, as well as the 3rd-century icon of the Assumption of Mary, which legend has it the saint brought back from the East.

THE ORDER OF MALTA'S KEYHOLE

Piazza dei Cavalieri di Malta
• Tel.: 06 5779193
• Metro: B - Circo Massimo

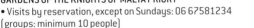

A surprising vision

The Piazza dei Cavalieri di Malta (Square of the Knights of Malta) is encircled by palm and cypress trees and flamboyant walls, rich in steles and obelisks, designed by Giovanni Battista Piranesi. The monumental entrance to the priory, headquarters of the Knights of Malta, seems to conceal a mysterious and unapproachable world but even the outside has a surprise in store.

By placing your eye to the keyhole of the main entrance, the dome of St Peter's Basilica can be seen, framed by an avenue of luxuriant greenery within the walled gardens. The Grand Prior Giovan Battista Rezzonico commissioned Piranesi to design the site, property of the Sovereign Order of Malta.

SIGHTS NEARBY

GARDENS OF THE KNIGHTS OF MALTA PRIORY

• Visits by reservation, except on Sundays: 06 67581234
(groups: minimum 10 people)

The origins of the priory date back to the 10th century, when as Santa Maria Aventina it formed part of a Benedictine abbey dedicated to Saint Basil of Cappadocia. In the 12th century the abbey passed into the hands of the Templars and, at the beginning of the 14th century, to the Knights of Rhodes – later known as the Knights of Malta.

Today, you can overcome the frustration born of peering through the priory

keyhole (see above), as group visits can be booked to tour the priory and its grounds.

Access is by a magnificent although relatively small garden, whose exoticism gives it a heady air of romance. In one corner of the garden a well built by the Templars still survives, the only vestige of their passing.

You can also visit the church of Santa Maria del Priorato, built in the 16th century. It is the only architectural work – apart from the piazza – carried out by Piranesi himself.

The single-nave interior has been entirely covered in white stucco to his design, and the façade offers a typical example of Piranesian style.

THE ORDER OF MALTA: THE ONLY PRIVATE INSTITUTION IN THE WORLD WITH THE ATTRIBUTES OF A SOVEREIGN STATE – EXTRATERRITORIALITY, EMBASSIES …

The Sovereign Military and Hospitaller Order of St John of Jerusalem, of Rhodes, and of Malta, more commonly known down the ages as Knights Hospitaller, Order of the Knights of Rhodes, and Order of Malta, is one of the most ancient Roman Catholic religious orders whose current mission is to defend the faith and assist the poor and needy.

Founded in Jerusalem around 1050 by merchants of the former republic of Amalfi to care for pilgrims in the Holy Land, this monastic community dedicated to John the Baptist was recognised as a religious order by Pope Paschal II in 1113.

The Hospitallers rapidly became militarised after the taking of Jerusalem during the First Crusade of 1099, second only to the Templars as a fighting force in the Holy Land. After the fall of Jerusalem and Saint Jean d'Acre in 1291, the Order retreated to Cyprus from 1291 to 1309. As the knights' rivalry with the King of Cyprus was creating difficulties, they conquered the island of Rhodes, then under Byzantine rule, and made it their new headquarters in 1310, ruling there until 1523. The island situation led them to acquire a fleet that became the scourge of Muslim shipping. Eventually vanquished by the Turks, the knights sailed to Civitavecchia and then Viterbe, in Italy, before travelling to Nice and in 1530 finally settling in Malta, given to them by the Holy Roman Emperor Charles V who had understood how useful they could be against any Ottoman advances. But Napoleon drove them out when he occupied the island in 1798, and they were finally welcomed in Rome by the pope in 1834.

Before the loss of Malta, most members of the order were monks who had taken the three vows of poverty, chastity and obedience. Even today some members are monks, but most of the knights and dames that now make up the Order are lay members (there are 11,000 of them). The military function has not been exercised since 1798.

Although, in the past, the knights of the Order had to come from chivalrous and noble Christian families, current members need only distinguish themselves by their faith, morality and the virtues sought within the Church and the Order itself. Although volunteers are always welcome, you can only become a member by invitation.

The Order maintains diplomatic relations with 100 countries through its embassies. It has a very special status, making it the only private institution that is treated almost like a country in itself. Activities are financed by donations from members and other private parties.

Its headquarters are at two sites in Rome, which have been granted extraterritoriality. These are Palazzo di Malta at 68 Via dei Condotti, where the grand master resides and meets with government bodies, and Villa Malta on the Aventine Hill, which houses the Grand Priory of Rome, the Embassy of the Order to the Holy See and the Embassy of the Order to the Italian Republic.

THE MALTESE CROSS

Founded in 11th-century Jerusalem by merchants from Amalfi (near Naples, the Sovereign Order of the Knights Hospitaller of St John of Jerusalem (the future Knights of Malta) first took the symbol of Amalfi's port (without its blue background) to be theirs. Then, in 1130, Raymond de Puy converted the charitable brotherhood into a military Order and won the right to use a white cross from Pope Innocent II; the colour was chosen to avoid confusion with the Templars' red cross. Shortly after the Turks drove them off the island of Rhodes in 1523, the Order settled on Malta. At that point, the island's red flag, inherited from the period of Norman occupation, became the background to the white cross, thus creating the Maltese Cross.

THE MEANING OF THE EIGHT POINTS IN THE MALTESE CROSS

The eight points in the Maltese Cross signify various things:
- the eight sides of the Dome of the Rock at Jerusalem.
- the eight nationalities of the original knights of the Order of St John of Jerusalem (the future Order of Malta) or the eight principles they undertook to live by: spirituality, simplicity, humility, compassion, justice, pity, sincerity and patience.
- the eight virtues which a knight of the Order of Malta was expected to possess: loyalty, pity, frankness, courage, honour, contempt of death, solidarity with the sick and poor, respect for the Catholic Church.
- the Eight Beatitudes which Christ listed in his Sermon on the Mount (St Matthew's Gospel, Chapter 5):

Blessed are the poor in spirit: for theirs is the kingdom of heaven. (Verse 3)

Blessed are the meek: for they shall possess the land. (Verse 4)

Blessed are they who mourn: for they shall be comforted. (Verse 5)

Blessed are they that hunger and thirst after justice: for they shall have their fill. (Verse 6)

Blessed are the merciful: for they shall obtain mercy. (Verse 7)

Blessed are the clean of heart: for they shall see God. (Verse 8)

Blessed are the peacemakers: for they shall be called the children of God. (Verse 9)

Blessed are they that suffer persecution for justice' sake, for theirs is the kingdom of heaven. (Verse 10)

THE PROTESTANT CEMETERY

6 Via Caio Cestio
- Tel: 06 5741900
- Tram: 3
- Metro: B – Piramide
- Open 9am-4pm from 1 October to 31 March, and 9am-5:30pm from 1 April to 30 September

> *"Here Lies One Whose Name is Writ in Water."*

Beside the Cestia Pyramid (the great imitation of the ancient Egyptian pyramids), built as a mausoleum by Caio Cestio, rises an old cemetery protected by pine and cypress trees and by ancient Roman walls. A hidden corner of tranquility, it is one of the most romantic places in the city.

This cemetery, in which about four thousand people of every race and creed are buried, has many names: the English Cemetery, due to the fact that the majority of the deceased are of English nationality, the Artists and Poets' Cemetery, not just because of the very large number of artists and poets buried there, but also because of the fact that so many artists and poets have loved it and sung its praises, and finally, probably the most correct name is that of Protestant Cemetery.

What surprises most while strolling along its paths, however, is the magic atmosphere that predominates, the distinctive appeal, the feeling of calm and serenity that make you think that perhaps, in such a place eternal sleep is not so bad.

The cemetery is divided in two by a wall and a ditch. The more recent part has an impressive number of graves, scattered among the trees and covered with flowers planted everywhere, amongst which that of the great English poet Percy Bysshe Shelley, for example, who drowned at the age of thirty on Viareggio beach, and those of August Von Goethe, Johann Wolfgang's natural son, the famous poet Carlo Emilio Gadda and Antonio Gramsci. The older part of the cemetery is different, yet nonetheless still striking, its few graves almost disappearing under the grass of the first piece of land given to the pope in 1722 to bury the Protestants inside the city walls (a practice that was not allowed until then). The grave of another very young English poet is also here: John Keats, who was misunderstood while alive, asked to have the following inscription put on his headstone: "Here Lies One Whose Name is Writ in Water."

THE MORTUARY CHAMBER OF PIRAMIDE DI CAIO CESTIO ❽

Piazza di Porta San Paolo (Ostiense)
• For reservations contact Pierreci
• Tel:06 39967700 (Mon-Sat 9am-1:30pm and 2:30pm-5pm)

> **You can go inside the pyramid ...**

The Pyramid of Gaius Cestius, which today forms part of the Aurelian Wall near the Porta San Paolo, is one of Rome's best-known and most unusual "minor" monuments.

The Roman taste for obelisks, sphinxes and sculptures from Egypt dates back to the 1st century BC. Temples dedicated to Isis and Serapis sprang up in the four corners of the empire and certain patricians even had the idea of erecting their own pyramid as a final resting place. Historical documents testify to the existence of at least three funerary pyramids in Rome.

Few people know, however, that the mortuary chamber of the Pyramid of Cestius, decorated with sumptuous frescoes, is open to the public.

Access to the monument is via a modern gallery. The interior consists of a single chamber measuring 4 by 6 metres, with a very austere barrel vault. A long gallery rises to the left. It was probably excavated in the Middle Ages by the first visitors to the tomb, hunting for treasure. At the time, the pyramid was partially buried, and the entrance was at a higher point than the original level.

The portrait of the deceased, Gaius Cestius, would have been displayed on the rear wall, or perhaps in the centre of the vaulting, but the looters must have taken it, leaving large holes in its place. Abundant graffiti also bear witness to the number of curious visitors, not to mention scholars such as Antonio Bosio, who entered the tomb at the beginning of the 17th century. Bosio was the first to scientifically analyse the city's forgotten underground structures, in particular the catacombs.

Among the many testimonies left by visitors is a drawing by one "Giorgio Bafaia Florentino".

The most striking feature, however, is the decoration of the main body (*cella*) of the monument. Some of the figures in the fresco painting stand out clearly from a white background, all executed with great finesse. Priestesses, amphoras and candelabras can be identified, as well as four superb Winged Victories on the vaulting – magnificent frescoes carried out in the purest Pompeian style.

LATERAN - COLOSSEUM - FORUM - CELIO

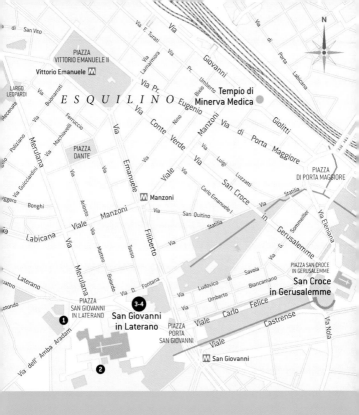

UNDERGROUND VAULTS OF SAINT JOHN'S HOSPITAL ❶

Complesso Ospedaliera San Giovanni-Addolorata
9 Via dell'Amba Aradam
• Visits by reservation
• Tel: 06 77053011
• E-mail: fpontoriero@sangiovanni.roma.it
• Admission: contributions welcome

Forgotten underground vaults

Although the underground vaults of the basilica of San Giovanni in Laterano (Saint John Lateran) are famous for the discovery of the remains of the barracks of Emperor Maxentius' imperial guard, many lesser-known structures dating back to the first four centuries of the Christian era lie beneath Saint John's Hospital.

Some of these buildings formed part of the *Domus Annorum*, the villa of Annius Verus, maternal grandfather of Marcus Aurelius, as borne out by the remains of lead water channels covered with inscriptions. The most striking feature is a grand arcaded peristyle, inside which can still be seen the ruins of marble pillars, capitals and gateways. Unfortunately nothing remains of the rich paving in rectangular marble slabs.

In the centre of the enclosure a large pool with a brick-lined base can still be distinguished. One of these bricks bears the imprint of a foot shod in *caligae*, the boots typically worn by Roman soldiers. The centre of the pool features a cement structure thought to be the pedestal of the equestrian statue of Marcus Aurelius that now stands in the Capitoline.

Until the 16th century, this statue stood in the middle of Piazza del Laterano, but there is nothing to prove that it was formerly within this rich residence.

Other excavations carried out in the late 1960s during the construction of a new building for the hospital revealed the remains of a number of structures dating from the 1st century BC to the 4th century AD. One of these has been identified as the villa of Licinius Sura, a hydraulic expert and friend of Tiberius. All the buildings in the area had to make way for the water supply, in particular the many aqueducts such as *aquæductus Celimontanus*, the arches of which can still be seen incorporated in the buildings of the square. On the walkways installed to let visitors view the site, you can admire the remains of fountains, garden drainage systems and water channels as well as the magnificent marble paving. The excavations finally revealed an enormous circular reservoir comprising four pools, built at a later date, filled with human bones, probably from the hospital, which was already in service during the Black Death of 1348.

NINE MEN'S MORRIS OR ESOTERIC SYMBOL?

The same grid, composed of three interlocking squares with four horizontal lines that stop short of the central square, can be found carved in many places in Europe, and even in China and Sri Lanka. Although some see this as just a board game known as Nine Men's Morris, it has been pointed out that this inscription has been found carved on vertical walls or reproduced on a very small scale, which would prevent it from being used as the basis for a game. Thus the grid is also thought to be an esoteric symbol used in spiritual quests, representing the three gradations on an initiate's path from the temporal to the sacred final goal, passing through the three worlds of the physical, intellectual, and spiritual or divine. It could also represent Heavenly Jerusalem with its twelve doors (three on each side of the grid). Used by the Knights Templar to mark sacred geographical sites or places where there was a particular concentration of physical and spiritual energy, the grid is also sometimes found in circular form. The circle initially would have corresponded to the beginning of the road while the square signified the culmination of the quest, hence the expression "squaring the circle" to symbolise the successful resolution of a problem.

Nine Men's Morris, also known as Mills or Merrills in English, has been played since antiquity (in Rome, Greece and Egypt). Two players each have nine pieces ("men") and take turns placing them on one of the board's twenty-four intersections. The object of the game is to align three pieces belonging to the same player. Sometimes ordinary pebbles of different colours are used.

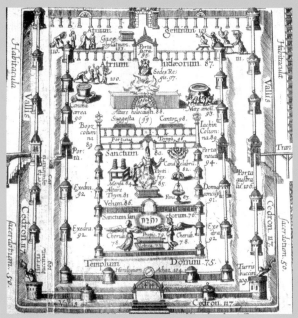

THE TRIPLE ENCLOSURES OF SAN GIOVANNI ❷
IN LATERANO CLOISTER

Cloister of San Giovanni in Laterano
• Open daily 9am-6pm
• Admission: €3
• Tel.: 06 77207991

> *Just
> a game,
> or an esoteric
> symbol?*

The superb cloister of San Giovanni in Laterano (Saint John Lateran), designed by Vassalletto in the 13th century, has three curious and discreet inscriptions within its grounds. Just to the right of the entrance is the first of these three markings, which some refer to as "triple enclosures".

There are two other sets of these interlocking squares in the cloister, this time traced vertically on the outer walls of the cloister. Numerous interpretations of these inscriptions exist (see below).

There are four places in Rome where such a grid can be seen: the basilicas of Santi Quattro Coronati, San Giovanni in Laterano, San Paulo Fuori le Mura, and San Lorenzo Fuori le Mura.

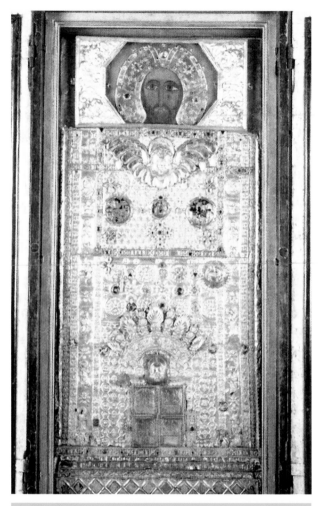

IS THE ARK OF THE COVENANT REALLY IN ETHIOPIA?

According to various sources, the Ark of the Covenant probably still exists. In *The Sign and the Seal: The Quest for the Lost Ark of the Covenant*, Graham Hancock recounts his search for the mythical Ark. After Jerusalem was invaded in the 6th century BC, the Ark is thought to have been taken across the Sinai Desert and along the Nile as far as Ethiopia, where it remains to this day, at Aksum. The almost magical influence of the Ark's presence might explain why Ethiopia is one of the few countries in the world that has never been totally colonised.

PRIVATE VISIT TO THE SANCTA SANCTORUM ❸

Piazza san Giovanni in Laterano
• Open Saturdays with prior booking at 10:30am, 12:30pm, 3pm and 4pm
• Tel.: 06 7726641

> ### Yes,
> ### you can enter
> ### the Holy
> ### of Holies

Contrary to common belief, the pope is not the only person authorized to enter the heart of the Sancta Sanctorum. On Saturdays anyone having pre-booked can visit this sanctuary, which is still held to be one of the most sacred in the Christian world, as borne out by the Latin inscription on the main fresco: "*Non est in toto sanctior orbe locus*" (There is no holier place in all the world).

In the former Temple of Solomon at Jerusalem, the term Sancta Sanctorum designated the most sacred part of the building, which housed the treasure of the temple as well as the mythical Ark of the Covenant containing the tablets of the Law of Moses, the rod of Aaron and the vial of manna from heaven (see opposite). Tradition dictated that only the High Priest had access to the Holy of Holies, once a year.

This sanctuary, now the pope's private chapel, was only accessible to a select few apart from the pontiff himself. Dedicated to Saint Lawrence, it was built by Pope Nicholas III in 1278. Many relics are preserved there, including a miraculous acheiropoietic image (not made by human hands) of Christ (see pages 140-141). Tradition holds that it was painted by Saint Luke himself, with the help of an angel. In the Middle Ages, the image was carried in procession to ward off the plague and other diseases. To prevent deterioration the image was covered with a layer of gold fitted with an opening for the face and little doors for the hands, feet and flank, which were opened at Easter for the worship of the five wounds of Christ's Passion.

In the following centuries, the image of Christ was damaged and was replaced by the copy we see today.

THE RELIC OF CHRIST'S FORESKIN   ❹

Sancta Sanctorum
• Open Saturdays with prior booking at 10:30am, 12:30pm, 3pm and 4pm
• Tel.: 06 7726641

> *Is the Holy Prepuce at the Lateran?*

According to Jewish tradition, Jesus was circumcised eight days after his birth. At a time when Christianity was fighting over the possession of holy relics, a great many far-fetched artefacts saw the light of day (see pages 138-139), including the foreskin of Christ. This is very likely to be one of the many faked relics and moreover one that is not recognised by the Church.

At Coulombs Abbey in France, a local belief attributes the holy relic with the power to make barren women fertile and give pregnant women an easy childbirth. This was why Catherine of Valois, the wife of King Henry V of England, had the relic brought to her in 1421 to ensure a successful birth.

In the Middle Ages, there were as many as fifteen different Holy Prepuces in Europe, although the one in Rome was the most renowned. It was said to have been offered as a wedding gift by the Byzantine empress, Irene the Athenian, and placed in the Sancta Santorum of the Lateran by the pope.

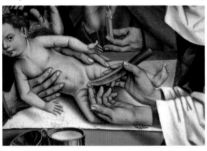

Several examples having been destroyed during the French Revolution, three other places of the original fifteen now claim the holy relic: Antwerp in Belgium, Conques and Vebret (Auvergne) in France.

MORE POWERFUL THAN THE HOLY FORESKIN, THE HOLY UMBILICAL CORD OF CHRIST!

At the height of the competition over holy relics (see pages 138-139), an improbable example was invented by unscrupulous merchants: the Holy Umbilicus, said to be the remains of Jesus' umbilical cord. This relic is preserved today at the church of San Giovanni in Laterano with another small fragment at Santa Maria del Popolo. Note that another Holy Umbilicus is thought to have existed at Châlons-en-Champagne, in France, until 1707, when the relic was destroyed by the bishop who judged it to be a fake. The town is said to have acquired the relic thanks to Charlemagne who himself received it from the Byzantine emperor. He was supposed to have given it to one of the popes, whose successor, probably the Frenchman Clement V, passed on a fragment to the bishop of Châlons.

GAME IN THE CLOISTER OF SANTI QUATTRO CORONATI BASILICA ❺

Santi Quattro Coronati Basilica
Via dei Santi Quattro Coronati
• Metro: Colosseo
• Cloister opening hours: 10am-11:45am (9:30am-10:30am on public holidays) and 4pm-5:45pm

Ancient game or measuring rod?

The basilica of Santi Quattro Coronati, although little known by the public, is one of the most charming and romantic religious buildings in Rome. The cloister, founded in the 13th century, is a marvel of beauty, sweetness and light, accentuated by the second-floor gallery and the double columns supporting it.

Just at the entrance to the cloister, on a low wall set between two rows of columns, fifteen parallel lines are carved into the stone, in the middle of which can be read signs that might be interpreted as Roman numerals. Some have seen this as a measuring rod or abacus from antiquity, others believe it was an ancient game resembling either snakes and ladders or dice, in which the number of points won depended on the distance from the two columns.

Almost opposite these lines on the other side of the cloister, there are more inscriptions, also subject to various interpretations. Two of these – the Nine Men's Morris and the esoteric symbol of the triple enclosure – have their supporters. The same inscription is found carved a second time on the wall of the cloister itself but has been almost obliterated.

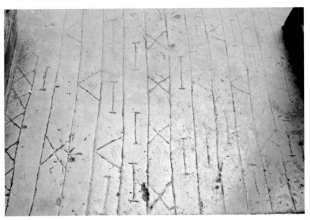

For more information on triple enclosures, see page 203.

VERBAL ABUSE IN BASILICA SAN CLEMENTE ⑥

- Open 9am-12:30pm and 3pm-6:30pm. Sundays from 10am
- Metro Colosseo

> ### Sons of whores, pull harder!

I n the Lower Basilica of San Clemente, the 11th-century frescoes showing Saint Clement celebrating Mass reveal a little-known episode in the life of the saint (bottom right of fresco).

The Roman prefect Sisinnius's wife Theodora, who had been converted to Christianity by Saint Clement, was beginning to spend a great deal of her time at church. Her husband, suspicious of her new faith, took her frequent absences as signs of infidelity and decided to follow her to find out what was going on, although she was simply attending Mass.

During the service, however, divine intervention struck down the jealous husband, rendering him deaf and blind. Theodora implored Saint Clement to heal her husband and the saint, praying to God, did so, but Sisinnius then got it into his head that the saint was a magician who had bewitched his wife in order to take advantage of her. So he ordered his servants to seize Clement and carry him away.

For the second time a miracle occurred: the servants, believing they had trussed up the saint, found that they had only managed to tie their ropes around a stout column. The fresco describes the exact moment when the exasperated Sisinnius, right, dressed in a toga, cries: "*Fili de le pute, traite!*" ["Pull harder, you sons of whores!"] – the terms of abuse are clearly visible on the fresco. One of the servants, Gosmari, repeats the order to another, Albertel: "*Albertel, traite*", who in turn asks a third fellow for help: "*Falite dereto co lo palo, Carvoncelle*" ["Carvoncelle, get behind with a lever"] – the inscription can still be seen bottom left.

Meanwhile, Clement, safely out of the way, comments on the scene in learned Latin: "*Duritiam cordis vestri saxa trahere meruisti*" ["You deserve to carry a great burden given the hardness of your hearts"].

THE LEGEND OF POPE JOAN

In an oratory at the junction of Via Santi Quattro and Via dei Querceti there is a painting in very poor condition that has often been interpreted as a memorial of the scandal of the legendary Pope Joan, who gave birth in the street. In fact it is simply a Virgin and Child.

The anti-papal satire of Pope Joan probably originated in popular culture during the 9th century and enjoyed great success in 13th and 14th-century court circles, although largely forgotten today.

It is said that on the death of Pope Leo IV, a young man from the German city of Mainz was elected pope under the title of John VIII and supposedly reigned from 853 to 855 (the pontificate of Leo IV in fact lasted until his death in 855, and Benedict III succeeded him a few weeks later). The young man in question was really a young girl who had just arrived in Rome disguised as a man, after studying in Athens. As she excelled in literary and scientific argument, she gained the respect of a number of academics. Still dressed in male attire, she quickly surrounded herself with followers and became so celebrated that she was made pope. Struggling with great difficulty against her natural desires, however, the young woman grew infatuated with a handsome cardinal, who at first was annoyed by the way she was looking at him. But his irritation melted as soon as he realised that the pope was really a young and beautiful Papessa. The two clerics wasted no time in becoming lovers and, uniquely in the history of the Church, the pope fell pregnant.

The story goes on to say that one day, on the processional route between the Lateran and Saint Peter's, the Papessa's waters broke and she gave birth in the middle of the road, near Saint Clement's church. The place is marked with a stone slab and the street, which no longer exists, came to be known as Vico della Papessa.

Pope Joan's name does not appear today on the list of holy pontiffs, in an attempt to eradicate the memory of this shameful incident. Moreover, the legend has it that thereafter it was stipulated that during a pope's consecration ceremony two cardinals must verify the sex of the new candidate by seating him on a seat with a hole in it, to check his attributes, and that after verification they should declare: "*Habet duos testiculos et bene pendentes*" (he has two well-hung testicles).

But this story was rather discredited by the existence of "commodes" manufactured long before the election of the Papessa.

The Church officially denied the legend in 1570, but it is said that until then the Easter processions carefully avoided the Vico della Papessa. In fact the papal processions never used that street.

IN QVESTE
PIETRE POSE
LE GINOCHIA S·PIETRO
QVANDO I DEMONII PORT·
SIMON MAGO
PER ARIA

THE MARKS OF SAINT PETER'S KNEES

Church of Santa Francesca Romana
Piazza Santa Francesca Romana
• Tel.: 06 6795528
• Opening times: 9:30am-12pm and 4pm-7pm

> *Prayer to interrupt the levitation of a sorceror*

Two stone slabs, worn down in the centre, are ensconced in the right wall of the transept of the church dedicated to Saint Frances of Rome (previously to Santa Maria Nuova), as you can see by ascending the two flights of stairs by the side of the crypt.

Tradition holds that these are the imprints left by Saint Peter's knees (or Saint Peter's and Saint Paul's, according to some sources) while praying to God to intervene against Simon Magus, who had levitated himself in the space above the Forum to show his superiority over the two Apostles. The prayer proved effective as the heretic fell to the ground and died on the spot.

Documents bearing witness to the life of Simon Magus have rarely been officially recognised, as the texts do not always agree and are largely derived from apocryphal sources, but according to the most popular version Simon was a magician or sorcerer from a small village in Samaria. On hearing Christian teaching, he requested baptism, although that did not stop him trying to bribe Saint Peter – who took it very badly – in order to acquire the privilege of transmitting the Holy Spirit by the laying on of hands.

It was precisely this legendary attempt by Simon Magus to commercialise spiritual gifts that gave rise to the term *simony*.

BLESSING MOTORISTS

Every year on 9 March a vast number of the faithful gather in their cars in Via dei Fori Imperiali and Piazza del Colosseo, trying their best to park as near to the church as possible to receive the solemn blessing bestowed in the name of Saint Frances of Rome.

This rich and noble lady lived in Rome until her death in 1440. She owed her fame to her generosity, having devoted her life to helping the poor and the sick. In 1425 she founded the Oblate Congregation of Tor de' Specchi (see page 69). She was declared a saint in 1608 and made patron saint of motorists in 1925.

Apparently motorists requested the protection of Saint Frances of Rome because a guardian angel had accompanied her throughout her "route" in life.

THE TABLE OF SANTA BARBARA ORATORY

Piazza di San Gregorio
• Open Tuesdays, Thursdays and Sundays 9:30am-12:30pm

> *Here*
> *Saint Gregory*
> *fed twelve*
> *paupers*
> *– and an angel*
> *joined them*
> *as thirteenth*
> *guest*

The surrounding wall of the splendid staircase leading to the church of San Gregorio al Celio is interrupted halfway up, on the left, by a gateway. You only need to go through this and ascend a few more steps to reach the site of three buildings: the oratories of Santa Barbara, Sant'Andrea and Santa Silvia.

It is said that the Barbara oratory was the former residence of Pope Saint Gregory I (Gregory the Great, 590-604) and that the sovereign pontiff had installed therein a large marble table on which he offered a daily meal to twelve paupers. One day, a thirteenth guest was present at the table – an angel who had taken on the guise of a poor man – and Gregory decided to feed him too. It is tempting to see in this person the figure of the traitor Judas, the thirteenth at the Last Supper, and to interpret Gregory's invitation as a call to love and forgive even those who betray us. Hence began the tradition, which persisted until 1870, to bring together thirteen guests at a meal offered by the pope each Holy Thursday, symbolising the pardoning of the traitor. The popular superstition that it is wiser to avoid seating thirteen at table is no less active today.

This very old oratory includes the ruins of a 3rd-century Roman building. It was restored on the initiative of Cardinal Baronio between 1602 and 1603. A marble statue representing Saint Gregory the Great bestowing a blessing, the work of Nicolas Cordier, stands in a niche. The walls are decorated with a series of frescoes attributed to Antonio Viviani carried out in 1603 and 1604, with scenes from the life of the pontiff.

The most striking object, in the centre of the chamber, is of course the large table, the very one where the twelve paupers ate. This massive structure in white marble, supported by two large stone griffons with a central palm tree, dates from the 3rd century AD. An inscription recalling the miracle of the angel reads: *Bissenos hoc Gregorius pascebat egentes – Angelus et decimus tertius accubuit* (Here Saint Gregory fed twelve paupers – and an angel joined them as thirteenth guest).

ORIGIN OF THE WORD "GROTESQUE"

When Nero died in 68 AD, his successors strived to eliminate the last traces of his extraordinary palace on the Esquiline, the famous Domus Aurea (Golden House).

The rooms, glittering with gold and precious stones and decorated with frescoes, marble sculptures and multi-coloured stucco, were looted and then buried up to the ceilings to serve as foundations for the imposing baths of Titus and Trajan. The lake in the valley below was drained and on its bed the Colosseum was erected.

The sumptuous frescoes of the Domus Aurea would thus remain hidden until their rediscovery in 1480, apparently quite by accident.

Legend has it that a young Roman fell into a crevice that had opened up on the Oppian Hill, to find himself in a kind of passageway with walls covered in painted figures. The news quickly spread and the prominent artists of the time, lovers of the arts of antiquity such as Pinturicchio, Ghirlandaio, Raphael, Giovanni da Udine, Filippino Lippi and Giulio Romano, were let down on ropes to look around what was thought at first to be caverns (grotte) and to copy the amazing decorations that covered every surface. For this reason, the decorations of the Domus Aurea and all those inspired by them over the following centuries (they were much in vogue throughout the 16th century) came to be known as *grottesche* (grotesques). Unfortunately those of the Domus Aurea have almost completely disappeared. Their rediscovery caused serious damage to the paintings and stuccos which, on exposure to the air and humidity, very quickly lost their colour.

The remains of the Domus Aurea were soon forgotten and excavations were only relaunched at the end of the 18th century after the discovery of the Pompeii frescoes.

This pictorial style did not meet with unanimous approval, however. It was often accused of being unseemly or ridiculous because of its brightly coloured fragile silhouettes painted in a calligraphic manner on a monochrome background devoid of perspective – rather monstrous hybrids with naturalistic effects in a geometric framework.

In time, these criticisms would give to the word "grotesque" a sense of the unusual and bizarre, extending to the caricatural or extravagant.

One of the artists who drew many grotesques was nicknamed "Morto" da Feltre because he had spent more time underground than on the surface, copying these strange ornamental motifs.

THE FIRST KNOWN GROTESQUE DECORATION OF THE RENAISSANCE

The church of Santa Maria del Popolo is home to a superb Pinturicchio painting, in the first chapel to the right of the main entrance. The painted decorations to each side of it are the first representation of grotesques following the discovery of the Domus Aurea.

THE MITHRAIC SANCTUARY OF CIRCO MASSIMO

9

16 Piazza della Bocca della Verità
• Visits on request, by telephoning the Cultural Heritage department of the Municipality of Rome (*Sovraintendenza Comunale ai Beni Culturali*) at 06 0608, alternatively through cultural associations such as *Roma Sotterranea* (www.romasotterranea.it)

> *One of the largest Mithraic sanctuaries in Rome*

In the early 1930s, during restoration work on the building facing the north-west of the Circo Massimo (Circus Maximus), at a depth of 14 metres below the present road level, the remains of a vast brick building from the 2nd century AD were discovered. Its location suggested a public building related to the neighbouring circus. This hypothesis is confirmed by the presence of a majestic flight of steps, a later addition leading to an upper storey.

In the 3rd century AD, certain ground-floor rooms were converted to house one of the largest Mithraic sanctuaries known in Rome (see page 223). Access is by a secondary entrance and a passage to the right, from which opens a service chamber.

A wide brick archway separates this chamber from the sanctuary proper, the sides of which are fitted with raised stone benches for use by worshippers. On the rear wall, a semi-circular niche probably held a statue of the god. The floor is paved with blocks of salvaged marble while in the centre

of the sanctuary stands a circular alabaster stone remarkable for its size. The scene is completed by an incredible white marble relief showing Mithras in the act of slaying a bull, surrounded by his two torch-bearers (*dadofori*) Cautes and Cautopates, the Sun, the Moon, a raven, a scorpion, a dog and a serpent.

OTHER MITHRAIC SANCTUARIES IN ROME

The sanctuary of Santa Prisca has some important paintings, a splendid effigy of the Sun god in *opus sectile* (composed of fragments of marble), and in a niche in the rear wall, the image of Mithras, unusually depicted naked, slaying the bull. An additional bonus is a reclining image of the god Saturn made with fragments of amphorae covered with stucco.

The sanctuary of San Clemente is located on the lowest level of the crypt of the church of the same name. The chamber is small in size and equipped with a central altar carved on all four sides. The vault, decorated with stucco stars, is pierced with eleven apertures: the largest, circular ones probably represent the seven planets of the solar system that were known at the time and which were associated with the seven grades of initiation, while four smaller rectangular openings feature the four seasons. At the back of the chamber, a niche houses a small statue of Mithras springing from the rock at his birth.

The sanctuary of the Palazzo Barberini park is unique because it features ten small paintings illustrating key episodes in the life of Mithras. These pictures frame a large painting of the tauroctony and the twelve signs of the zodiac.

The sanctuary of the Baths of Caracalla is the largest known in Rome. Roofed by large barrel vaults, the main chamber measures 23 by 10 metres. In the centre is a pit where an underground passage ends. This was thought to have been the *fossa sanguinis* of the sanctuary – the place where the initiate would lie prostrate during the ceremony in order to be doused with blood from the bull sacrificed in the hall overhead. This hypothesis seems dubious, however, given the practical difficulties of sacrificing such a large animal in these cramped and difficult to access caverns. This Mithraic sanctuary has retained its paving of white mosaic with a border of black tiles.

The sanctuary of the cellar of the church of Santo Stefano Rotondo is still decorated with a few frescoes of the Sun and Moon.

The sanctuary of Via Giovanni Lanza measures less than 6 m². Probably a site for private use, it was miraculously intact when discovered. The relief ornamentation, altar, oil lamps and antique vases were even in their original places ...

Sanctuary of Santa Prisca: 13 Via di Santa Prisca
Information and reservations from Pierreci at 06 39967700. Open 2nd and 4th Sundays of the month at 4pm for individual visits and at 3pm and 5pm for groups.

Sanctuary of San Clemente: 95 Via Labicana. Opening times: 9am-12:30pm and 3pm-6:30pm. Open Sundays at 10am. October until March until 6pm. Admission: € 6.

The sanctuaries of the Palazzo Barberini park, Santo Stefano Rotondo, Baths of Caracalla and Via Giovanni Lanza can only be visited through a number of cultural associations such as *Roma Sotterranea* (www.romasotterranea.it).

MITHRAISM – A FASCINATING ANCIENT CULT FOR INITIATES

Mithraism is a religion centred on Mithras, a god of Persian origin.

Mithras was born naked, springing from the living rock armed with a knife, a flaming torch in his hand, and a Phrygian cap on his head. A pact was signed after Mithras defeated the Sun. He thereby received the Sun's radiant crown, which became his emblem. In his tireless struggle against evil, with the help of his dog he captured and killed a bull, symbol of the impetuous animal forces that must be overcome. Grain miraculously spilled from the bull's wound, while its blood became the grapevine. Its death thus allowed rebirth... The evil spirit Ahriman, however, refused to admit defeat: he sent a scorpion and a serpent to attack Mithras, but to no avail. Mithras and the Sun then held a celebratory ritual meal known as an *agape*, a term still current today.

The cult of Mithras was usually celebrated in caves and grottoes, not because of any link with the powers of darkness, as some detractors would have it, but rather because the cave was a symbol of the cosmos, towards which believers tried to reach out during the ceremonies.

Mithras was flanked by two torch-bearers: Cautes and Cautopates, with whom he formed a triad (or Trinity). The first carried a lighted torch which represented the day, while the second carried an extinguished torch, pointing downwards, symbol of the night.

The concept of the soul's journey across the cosmos is key to all this: the way consisted of seven steps, linked to the seven planets, the seven days of the week, the seven metals and the seven stages of the soul which had to be gradually left behind. The cult was clearly a means of advancing on this path and progressively freeing oneself from passion. The *agape* feast, based on bread and wine, of course recalls the Eucharist, and the sacrifice

of the bull from which life sprang is a strange reminder of the crucifixion and resurrection ...

Mithraism spread to the West from the 1st century BC and was at its peak in the 3rd century AD, before being supplanted by Christianity.

CHRISTMAS OWES 25 DECEMBER TO THE WINTER SOLSTICE AND MITHRAISM ...

Contrary to widespread belief, no Christian scriptures actually claim that Jesus was born on the night of 24 to 25 December. The date of 25 December for Christ's birth was decreed in AD 354 by Pope Liberius to combat pagan Roman cults, and above all, Mithraism, which celebrated the birth of its god Mithras on 25 December to roughly coincide with the winter solstice (prior the Gregorian reform of the calendar, the winter solstice was not fixed and did not always fall on 21 December – which incidentally was one reason for the reform).

The appropriation of this date by the Church also allowed some very beautiful symbolism to develop: at the time of year when the days were shortest and night reigned supreme, the birth of Christ was a powerful symbol of day breaking once again, chasing away the shadows and heralding the resurrection.

Previously, Christians celebrated the birth of Christ on 6 January, the day of the Adoration of the Magi. Only the Armenian Apostolic Church still celebrates Christmas on that date. Orthodox faiths continue to commemorate Christmas on 25 December, but according to the Julian calendar, which differs by several days from the reformed Gregorian version.

Note also that Jesus was probably not born in AD 1, but sometime between 6 BC and AD 6...

ENRICO STURANI'S PRIVATE COLLECTION

14 Via del Cardello
• Tel: 06 486970
• Metro: B – Cavour or Colosseo
• Opening times: Prior reservation before visiting

140,000 postcards

Enrico Sturani, the owner of a unique and fascinating collection, warmly welcomes curious visitors, thus allowing them to discover the little known world of postcards. Along with numerous geography schoolbooks, this cultured man with an original personality has an exceptional collection of postcards in his unkempt apartment just a stone's throw from the Colosseum. This incredibly varied repertory of about 140,000 cards allows visitors to step back in time and go on an imaginary trip to the four corners of the world. All you have to do is ask and from the hundreds of cards that fill the shelves of every room, he will take out sometimes extraordinarily beautiful postcards dating from the beginning of the 20th century right up to recent times. Many of these cards come from France, New Zealand and other far away places.

It is almost impossible to find a subject, a year over the last century or a place that has escaped this passionate collector. From war cards to porn cards, from political cards to "lovers" cards, from those with animals to ones with chubby babies, both surreal and futuristic ones, everything becomes unexpectedly interesting especially with Mr Sturani's explanations, and the cards are a unique way of understanding the mentality, culture, tastes and psychology of people over the past hundred years.

TITULUS EQUITII BELOW THE BASILICA OF SAN MARTINO AI MONTI ⓫

Via Monte Oppio 28 (Celio)
• Visits on request, by contacting the cultural association *Roma Sotterranea* (www.romasotterranea.it)

> *One of the most interesting constructions of early Christian Rome*

O n the slopes of Colle Oppio, the basilica of San Martino ai Monti (Saint Martin of the Mountains) has one of the most interesting constructions of early Christian Rome preserved in its crypt.

Since excavations were carried out in 1637, a series of chambers has been discovered whose original use is disputed because of the numerous transformations they have undergone over the centuries.

On the outside, along Via Equizia, the change in level between apse and façade is offset by a massive wall composed of blocks of volcanic tufa, perhaps quarried from the ramparts known as the Mura Serviane (Servian Wall).

Once inside the church, you cross the central nave to a staircase leading down into a Baroque crypt beneath the main altar. From there, through a door to the left, is another stairway that gives access to a large rectangular brick-built hall, 14 by 17 metres, divided into three naves by six pillars. The original cladding is still there, with lattice vaults reinforced by concrete joists. This construction, which dates back to the 3rd century AD, used to be part of the neighbouring Baths of Trajan. Afterwards it was probably used for commercial purposes such as a covered market or a warehouse. Some scholars, however, believe it may have been a rich man's house (*domus*). From the late 3rd century, it is thought that it was used as a meeting place by the early Christians.

It was Pope Sylvester I (AD 314-335) who founded the basilica on this property, donated by one Equitius, hence the name *Titulus Equitii*, converting it to the requirements of the Christian rite at communal meetings.

It soon became a site of major importance for the Christian Church: the Synods of AD 499 and AD 595 were both held here.

The church above was built in the 9th century, and the crypts were restored and embellished at the same time. Certain sections of painting that can still be seen on the vaulting are from this period: scenes of saints surrounded by the Virgin and Jesus, whose postures and strikingly coloured clothing are typical of Byzantine art.

Fragments of mosaic are also visible on the black-and-white paving, which along with the ornamental motifs of some of the frescoes, seems to date from the early 3rd century, at the time when the site was still in commercial use.

A second flight of steps leads to other underground chambers, unfortunately completely buried.

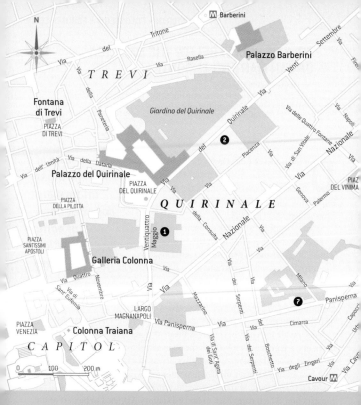

QUIRINALE -TERMINI -
MONTI - ESQUILINO

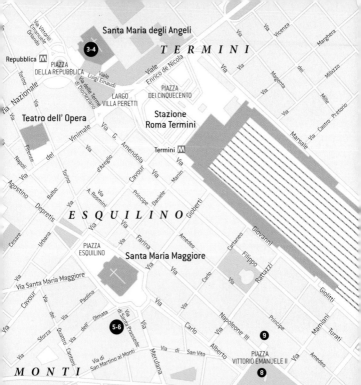

CASINO DELL'AURORA

Palazzo Pallavicini-Rospigliosi
43 Via XXIV Maggio
• Tel: 06 83467000
• Opening times: First day of the month, 10am-12pm and 3pm-5pm
• Admission: Free • Private visits: Every day, group of 20 people minimum
• Admission: €15 per person on weekdays and €20 per person on public holidays • Specialised foreign language guides available on request

> *See the dawn once a month*

I n the grounds of the extraordinary Palazzo Pallavicini-Rospigliosi, the Casino dell'Aurora (Dawn Pavilion) is open to the public free of charge on the first day of every month. The palace, built in 1610 over the ruins of the Baths of Constantine, was the former home of the powerful Cardinal Mazarin (Giulio Mazzarino). The *casino* (pavilion), designed at the same time as the hanging garden and the semicircular fountain on the opposite side, was built by the Flemish cabinet-maker Giovanni Vasanzio (the Italian name of Jan Van Santen), who became the assistant of the celebrated architect Flaminio Ponzio upon arriving in Rome. The building's two levels are only visible on the outside from Via XXIV Maggio, because on the other side, which faces the garden, the lower level is buried due to the difference in height between street and garden. The building, which on both levels consists of a central hall flanked by two smaller rooms, has the typical "C" form of hunting lodges and suburban villas built from the end of the 15th century, and the garden side corresponds to the second floor of the building reserved for banquets and formal ceremonies. On the ceiling of the central hall is the fresco masterpiece that gives the pavilion its name: *Aurora* by Guido Reni, painted 1613-1614, and one of the most copied works in the history of art over the past four centuries. The central hall is filled with 17th-century marble busts of Roman emperors and famous Greek statues, such as *Artemis the Huntress* and the *Rospigliosi Athena*.

PRIVATE VISIT: THE SIDE ROOMS OF CASINO DELL'AURORA

By booking (Madame Capaccioli at 06 83467000), not only can you visit the pavilion in peace but also gain access to two side rooms that are closed during the monthly public tours.

The ceilings are frescoed with Giovanni Baglione's *Renaldo and Armida* and Passignano's *Battle of Armida*. There are also two paintings by Guido Reni, *Christ Crucified* and *Andromeda Freed by Perseus*, as well as *The Death of Julian the Apostate* and *The Conversion of Saul* by Luca Giordano.

PAVILION OF THE MUSES

Exceptionally it may also be possible to visit the Pavilion of the Muses, which forms part of the same palace complex. Some very fine frescoes can be seen there by Orazio Gentileschi and Agostino Tassi. Reservation again through Madame Capaccioli at 06 83467000.

THE STATUE OF *STANISLAS KOSTKA*

Church of San Andrea al Quirinale
29 Via del Quirinale
• Tel.: 06 4744872
• Open Monday to Friday 8:30am-12pm and 3:30pm-7pm, and Saturday and Sunday 9am-12pm and 4pm-7pm

> *A marvellous statue embedded in a picture frame*

Most visitors to San Andrea al Quirinale, who restrict themselves to the main church precinct, will not suspect they are missing the best part: at the back of the church a passage to the right leads into a corridor where postcards and other souvenirs are sold.

From there you can enter the two most interesting places in the building, but you need to know about them because they are usually closed. You only have to ask, however, and the door to the superb sacristy will be opened.

This room, with a beautiful richly frescoed ceiling, can be admired with the help of the lamps that will be lit for you, but we recommend investing 50 centimes in some extra lighting to see it better. For the modest sum of one euro, you can also ask to see the rooms housing the relics of Saint Stanislas Kostka on the first floor of the building (home of the Jesuit seminary). Born in Poland in 1550 and dead by the age of 18 in 1568, Stanislas Kostka entered the Jesuits novitiate in Rome when he was 16, after studying in Vienna. Against the wishes of his father, he had run away from home in 1567 and crossed the whole of Germany on foot. In the second room is a quite extraordinary and neglected sculpture by Pierre Legros the Younger, dating from 1702 to 1703. In spectacular detail, it shows the saint lying on his deathbed in a superb blend of polychrome marble that captures the smallest folds in the draperies. The black marble tunic he is wearing is incredible enough: more like a 19th-century

dandy's coat than a religious habit, it means that the saint had not yet been ordained as a priest.

You will also notice the curious detail that a section from the painting behind the marble bed has been cut out. This work by Tommaso Minardi depicting the Holy Virgin, Saint Barbara, Sainte Cecilia and Saint Agnes welcoming the saint, was hung after the Legros sculpture was in place. As the statue touched the wall, a section of the frame had to be removed to fit in the painting, which is of little interest in itself.

THE SUNDIAL OF SANTA MARIA DEGLI ANGELI CHURCH

3

Piazza delle Repubblica
• Metro: B - Repubblica
• Open Saturdays, 7:30am-6:30pm, and Sundays, 8:30am-7:30pm

A testimonial to momentous reform

Santa Maria degli Angeli (Our Lady of the Angels) is a majestic basilica built within the Baths of Diocletian according to designs by Michelangelo, with later additions by Vanvitelli.

On the floor of the basilica in front of Diaz's tomb, one can admire a very beautiful sundial measuring 45 metres long, also called the *Linea Clementina* (Clementine Line) since it was inaugurated by Pope Clement XI on 6 October 1702.

This beautiful bronze and marble inlay had become rather worn after centuries of being tread upon by churchgoers, but restoration work in 2000 rendered it all its former beauty.

Its creation dates back to 1700, when, in order to check the accuracy of the Gregorian reform of the calendar, Pope Clement XI asked the mathematician and astronomer Francesco Bianchini to build a monumental sundial that would indicate the spring equinox and therefore help to determine the exact date of Easter Sunday.

According to the rules set out by the Fathers of the Church at the Council of Nicaea in 325, Easter was to be celebrated on the first Sunday after the first full moon following the spring equinox. Therefore it was extremely important to avoid mistakes that would have inevitably moved the dates of all the other movable religious holidays.

Alongside the sundial is another old marble inlay representing the signs

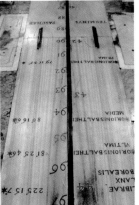

of the Zodiac. These were based on Maratta's drawings, using the images of Bayer's *Uranometria Nova*.

To the right of the line, the signs of summer and autumn constellations appear; to the left, those of spring and winter. Every day of the year at midday, the rays of the sun, entering the building through the centre of the heraldic coat of arms of Pope Clement XI, touch a different point of the line, advancing from Cancer during the summer solstice to Capricorn during the winter solstice, and then back through the rest of the signs to Cancer.

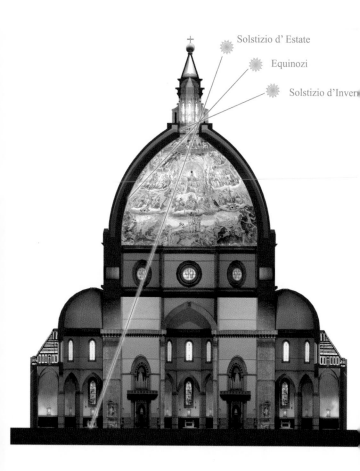

Solstizio d' Estate

Equinozi

Solstizio d'Inver

HOW DOES A MERIDIAN WORK?

Instead of using the shadow of a gnomon, meridians use a small hole placed at a certain height, through which the sun's light falls onto a meridian line (i.e. one aligned exactly north-south). The fact that the sun's rays perform the function of the shadow in a traditional sundial means that the opening is sometimes referred to as a "gnomonic opening".

The higher the opening, the more efficient the meridian, hence the interest in using cathedrals (see p. 241 "Why where meridians installed in cathedrals?"); the circumference of the hole had to be no more than one thousandth of the height above the ground. Obviously, the opening had to be installed on the south side of the building in order to let in the rays of the sun, which lies to the south in the northern hemisphere.

The meridian line should run from the point which stands perpendicularly below the axis of the opening, not always easy to determine using the instruments available to scientists in the past. The length of the line depends on the height of the opening; in some cases, where the building was not long enough to trace the entire meridian line across the floor (as was the case at Saint-Sulpice in Paris), an obelisk was added at its end, so that the movement of the sun's rays could then be measured up the vertical. In summer, when the sun is highest in the sky, the sun's rays fall onto the meridian line closer to the south wall (where that line begins) than they do in winter, when the sun is lower over the horizon and the rays tend to strike towards the far end of the meridian line.

The main principle behind the working of the meridian is that at noon, solar time, the sun is at its apex and, by definition, its rays fall straight along a line running exactly north-south. So, the exact moment when those rays strike the meridian line, which does run north-south, indicates the solar noon.

Furthermore, the exact place on the meridian line where the rays fall makes it possible to determine the day of the year: the point right at the beginning of the line is reached solely on the day of the summer solstice, while the exact end of the line is reached on the day of the winter solstice. Experience and observation meant that the meridian line could be calibrated to identify different days of the year.

Once this was done, the line could be used to establish the date of various movable feasts, such as Easter – one of the great scientific and religious uses of meridians. Similarly, the different periods corresponding with the signs of the Zodiac could be established, which explains why such signs are indicated along the length of a number of meridian lines.

WHY WAS 4 OCTOBER FOLLOWED IMMEDIATELY BY 15 OCTOBER IN THE YEAR 1582?
THE MEASUREMENT OF TIME AND THE ORIGIN OF THE MERIDIANS

The entire problem of the measurement of time and the establishment of calendars arises from the fact that the Earth does not take an exact number of days to orbit the sun: one orbit in fact takes neither 365 nor 366 days but rather 365 days, 5 hours, 48 minutes and 45 seconds.

At the time of Julius Caesar, Sosigenes of Alexandria calculated this orbit as 365 days and 6 hours. In order to make up for this difference of an extra 6 hours, he came up with the idea of an extra day every four years: thus the Julian calendar – and the leap year – came into being.

In AD 325, the Council of Nicaea established the temporal power of the Church (it had been called by Constantine, the first Roman emperor to embrace Christianity). The Church's liturgical year contained fixed feasts such as Christmas, but also movable feasts such as Easter. The latter was of essential importance as it commemorated the death and resurrection of Christ, and so the Church decided that it should fall on the first Sunday following the full moon after the spring equinox. That year, the equinox fell on 21 March, which was thus established as its permanent date.

However, over the years, observation of the heavens showed that the equinox (which corresponds with a certain known position of the stars) no longer fell on 21 March... The 11 minute and 15 second difference between the real and assumed time of the Earth's orbit around the sun was resulting in an increasing gap between the actual equinox and 21 March.

By the 16th century, that gap had increased to ten full days and so Pope Gregory XIII decided to intervene. Quite simply, ten days would be removed from the calendar in 1582, and it would pass directly from 4 October to 15 October. It was also decided, on the basis of complex calculations (carried out most notably by the Calabrian astronomer Luigi Giglio), that the first year of each century (ending in 00) would not actually be a leap year, even though divisible by four. The exceptions would fall every 400 years, which would mean that in 400 years there would be a total of just 97 (rather than 100) leap years. This came closest to making up the shortfall resulting from difference between the real and assumed time of orbit. Thus 1700, 1800 and 1900 would not be leap years, but 2000 would...

In order to establish the full credibility of this new calendar – and convince the various Protestant nations that continued to use the Julian calendar – Rome initiated the installation of large meridians within its churches. A wonderful scientific epic had begun...

The technical name for a leap year is a bissextile year. The term comes from the fact that the additional day was once placed between 24 and 25 February. In Latin, 24 February was the sixth (*sextus*) day before the calends of March, hence the name *bis sextus*, to indicate a supplementary sixth day. The *calends* were the first day of each month in the Roman calendar.

THE MERIDIAN OF SANTA MARIA DEL FIORE: THE HIGHEST MERIDIAN IN THE WORLD

From the 15th to the 18th centuries almost 70 meridians were installed in churches in France and Italy. Only nine, however, have a gnomonic opening that is more than 10 metres above floor level – that height being crucial to the accuracy of the instrument:

S. Maria del Fiore (Florence)	90.11 m
S. Petronio (Bologna)	27.07 m
St-Sulpice (Paris)	26.00 m
Monastery of San Nicolo l'Arena (Catania, Sicily)	23.92 m
Cathedral (Milan)	23.82 m
S. Maria degli Angeli (Rome)	20.34 m
S. Giorgio (Modica, Sicily)	14.18 m
Museo Nazionale (Naples)	14.00 m
Cathedral (Palermo)	11.78 m

WHY WERE MERIDIANS INSTALLED IN CATHEDRALS?

To make their measurements more precise, astronomers required enclosed spaces where the point admitting light was as high as possible from the ground: the longer the beam of light, the more accurately they could establish that it was meeting the floor along an exactly perpendicular plane. Cathedrals were soon recognised as the ideal location for such scientific instruments as meridians. Furthermore, the Church had a vested interest as well, because meridians could be used to establish the exact date of Easter.

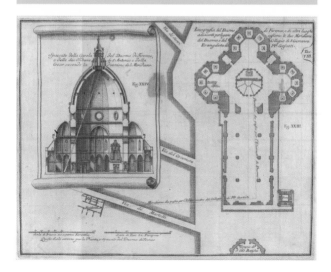

STELLAE POLARIS ORBITA

23

22

X

X

V

X

THE BOREAL MERIDIAN OF SANTA MARIA DEGLI ANGELI CHURCH

Piazza delle Repubblica
• Metro: B – Repubblica
• Open on Saturdays 7:30am-6:30pm and on Sundays 8:30am-7:30pm

> **The only meridian in the world for tracking the pole star**

Although the solar meridian of Santa Maria degli Angeli is relatively well known, the extraordinary boreal meridian also found in the transept of this church is much less so. Oriented north, in contrast to the sundial which is oriented south, this boreal meridian is the only known example of its kind.

It is intended to track on the church floor the movement around the North

Pole of the pole star (Polaris), which can be seen through a hole located high up (27.20 m) on the right wing of the church. Near the beginning of the solar meridian seventeen magnificent ellipses correspond to the various trajectories of the star. This boreal meridian is an extraordinary and rare instrument that makes it possible to measure the effect of the precession of the equinoxes (see below).

Other than its astronomical function, Bianchini's meridian also marks the midnight hour, corresponding to the beginning of the ecclesiastical day (see also pages 240-241).

WHERE DOES THE WORD "BOREAL" COME FROM?

In Greek mythology, Boreas was the son of Eos and Astraeus and personified the north wind. The adjective boreal, by extension, denotes the north or northern regions.

Further detail on the operation of the two meridians of Santa Maria degli Angeli church can be found in the remarkable book *Il cielo in Basilica* (Italian only, Agami publishers).

THE FLOGGING PILLAR OF SANTA PRASSEDE ❺

Santa Prassede Basilica
9 Via di Santa Prassede / Via di San Martino ai Monte
• Tel.: 06 4882456
• Metro: Cavour or Vittorio Emmanuele
• Open daily 7:30am-12pm and 4pm-6:30pm

> *The pillar on which Christ is said to have been flogged*

To the right of the superb chapel of Saint Zeno, an antechamber is home to an astonishing fragment of the pillar on which Christ is said to have been flogged and tortured during his Passion.

The relic is thought to have been housed here since the 13th century. It appeared for the first time in Jerusalem in the 5th century, according to pilgrims' accounts. It has changed form several times judging by various testimonies, probably as a result of being stolen, lost, sold, and reinvented, like many other holy relics (see pages 138-139). The pillar was originally described as a simple column of stone. Later, certain pilgrims swore that the imprints of Jesus' hands could be seen on it, and in the 6th century, it was even affirmed that the arms and face of Christ were imprinted on the stone.

Jerusalem, Padua, Ancona, Venice and Toledo also claim to possess fragments of the pillar.

At the entrance to Saint Zeno's chapel, opposite the little souvenir shop, is a painting that lets you envisage how the pillar was put to use during the Passion.

THE SQUARE HALO OF SANTA PRASSEDE BASILICA ❻

Santa Prassede Basilica
9 Via di Santa Prassede / Via di San Martino ai Monte
• Tel.: 06 4882456
• Metro: Cavour or Vittorio Emmanuele
• Open daily 7:30am-12pm and 4pm-6:30pm

> *Square halos were for subjects alive at the time a mosaic was created*

Santa Prassede Basilica, famous for its mosaic cycles made by Byzantine artists in the 9th century, was erected by command of Pope Paschal I (817-824) in honour of Saint Praxedes, the sister of Saint Pudentiana and daughter of Saint Pudens, with whom Saint Peter is said to have stayed. She is also mentioned in the Epistles of Paul. The celebrated mosaic in the apse depicts Saints Praxedes and Pudentiana ascending to heaven. To the right of Jesus, Praxedes stands between Saint Zeno and Pope Paschal I, who is presenting Christ with a model of the church he had had built. You will notice that his head is encircled by a very unusual halo: square and blue, instead of the traditional round golden halo (see box below). Similarly, Paschal's mother Theodora, who is buried in the Saint Zeno chapel, is shown above the door on the left, inside the chapel, also wearing a square blue halo.

This type of halo can also be seen in the mosaics of the church of Santa Cecilia in Trastevere, again surrounding the head of Paschal I, who was the force behind the rebuilding of this church too. Outside the Basilica of Saint John Lateran, the apse mosaic of the remains of Leo III's papal dining hall (*Triclinium Leoninum*) also depicts the pope (795-816) with a square halo.

WHY SQUARE HALOS?

Until the 4th century, only Christ wore a halo, the symbol of those who lived as saints and who had been admitted to heaven. From the 9th century, the halo would nevertheless be accepted for all the saints. These were plain round haloes, the circle being a symbol of perfection and eternity, and golden in colour, symbol of divine light. Haloes are often interpreted as representations of the heavenly space (the aura, in more modern terms) that surrounds the saints. It is focused on the head, supposed to be the noblest part of the human body, the seat of the soul.

The square halo that surrounds certain figures in mosaics signifies that the person was alive at the time the mosaic was made. It represents the earth and the four points of the compass. Blue, the colour of the sky, is the most spiritual, the purest and closest to the divine. It symbolises self-detachment and the flight of the soul towards God and thus indicates an intermediate stage on the path to God and the colour gold.

MUSEO DI PATOLOGIA DEL LIBRO

76 Via Milano
- Open by appointment.
- Tel.: 06 48291 – 48291304 – 48291235
- E-mail: icplform@tin.it
- Admission free

> **Books may suffer, but they will be well looked after**

The little-known Museum of Book Pathology was set up in 1938 on the initiative of the Museo dell'Istituto Centrale di Patologia del Libro (Central Institute for Book Pathology). Since then, it has assiduously built up a collection illustrating how books are manufactured and how they eventually deteriorate.

The museum has now been completely refurbished on a new site. A particular attempt has been made to promote a collection of one-of-a-kind objects via a tour laid out in three sections. The first section is devoted to the production materials and techniques of both ancient and modern books. The second covers the various ways in which books can be damaged, and the third their conservation and restoration.

Thanks to the experience acquired by the museum staff and the collaboration of the Institute's laboratories, it has been possible to make new teaching aids available to the public that actively encourage visitor participation, making the tour much more interesting for adults as well as for children.

The average length of the museum visit is around 45 minutes. Audio guides in Italian or English are available for all age groups. A series of panels provide a short introduction to each section, while a video illustrates the work of the Institute. There is also an educational workshop entirely devoted to younger children.

THE MARQUIS OF PALOMBARA'S PORTA ALCHEMICA ❽

Piazza Vittorio Emanuele II
• Tram: 5, 14
• Metro: A – Vittorio Emanuele

Gateway to gold ?

The Porta Alchemica, also called the Magic Portal, Alchemy Gate or Heaven's Gate, is an esoteric monument covered with astrological and alchemical symbols intermingled with equally hermetic phrases in Latin and Hebrew. Erected in 1680, as indicated by the inscription, this Porta Alchemica is the only survivor of the five gates of Villa Palombara, the residence of Massimiliano Palombara, Marquis of Pietraforte (1614–1680). The villa was demolished in the late 19th century when the railway station was expanded and, in 1873, the door was dismantled before being rebuilt nearby in 1888, on a former wall of Saint Eusebius Church in the gardens of what is now Piazza Vittorio. This was when the two statues of the Egyptian god Bes, which once stood at the Quirinal Palace, were added to either side of the door. This minor ancient Egyptian deity was believed to protect the home against harmful spirits, and thus to be a protector of sleep, fertility and marriage. These attributes and his traditional image contribute to his similarity to the god of the gnomes, which the ancient hermetists called Gob or Gobi. Above the door is a medallion showing an orb (a globe topped with a cross) superimposed over a six-branched star, commonly called the "Star of David", which represents the perfect harmony between the heavens (bottom triangle) and the earth (inverted triangle). At the centre of the first circle is another smaller circle in the shape of a stylised rose which, along with the cross, is a reminder of the Rose+Croix esoteric movement. The various Latin phrases and astrological symbols scattered across the door are symbolic references to the Rosicrucian path of spiritual illumination, which is equivalent to obtaining the philosopher's stone for alchemists. The Holy Spirit, through its incarnation as man, allows man to reach perfect harmony within himself: the balance between aggression and restraint or between his feminine and masculine instincts. Senator Massimiliano Palombara was a true follower of alchemy as well as a member of the Rosicrucian Order. The medallion above the door, the only remaining trace of his palace, is identical to that found on the cover of the alchemical treatise "Aureum Saeculum Redivivum" (The Golden Age Restored) by Henricus Madatanus (pseudonym of Adrian von Mynsicht, 1603–1638), who was also a Rosicrucian. The cover of the original edition of this 1621 work is quite different from that of the posthumous 1677 edition that inspired Palombara. According to the legend collected in 1802 by specialist Francesco Girolamo Cancellieri, one night the Marquis Palombara welcomed a passing pilgrim to his palace, a pilgrim who, unknown to Palombara, was a Rosicrucian Master. Some believe the man was alchemist Francesco Giustiani Bono, who gave his disciple a powder capable of producing gold, as well as a mysterious manuscript filled with esoteric symbols that contained the secret of the philosopher's stone. These symbols could well be those engraved around the door, which, by the way, was the one through which the mysterious wise man disappeared the next morning, never to be seen again.

BLESSING OF THE ANIMALS AT SANT'EUSEBIO

9

Sant'Eusebio church
Piazza Vittorio Emanuele II
• Tram: 5, 14
• Metro: A – Vittorio Emanuele

Bless your pet, horse or cow...

E very year on 17 January, people have their animals blessed in front of this church. This used to happen in front of the church on Via Carlo Alberto dedicated to Saint Anthony the abbot, protector of animals, but the function was transferred to the front of Sant'Eusebio church because of traffic problems.

Although today this centuries-old tradition only concerns pets, in the past it was a rite concerning all animals, including horses, cows and other farmyard animals. Farmers having their animals blessed had to bring an offering in kind to the church, whereas nobles were asked for money, donations of various other types and large candles which were said to protect the animals from all harm.

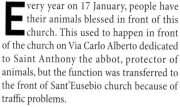

In fact, the number of nobles asking for private services for their animals excessively increased the amounts of money linked to the blessing, so other parishes tried to organise similar ceremonies in their churches. The phenomenon grew to such an extent that it finally forced the cardinal vicar in 1831 to threaten to suspend *a divinis* any priests who carried out blessings on animals without permission.

OUTSIDE THE CENTRE

THE CANNON BALL IN THE AURELIAN WALL ❶
Via Pio

> *Souvenir of the taking of Rome*

I n the section of the Aurelian Wall beyond Porta Pinciana, the tower overlooking Via Pio holds a startling reminder of the 1870 battle that seems to pass unnoticed. A cannonball is quite simply and spectacularly embedded in the wall.

The nearby Porta Pia is renowned for the fighting of 20 September 1870, the day when the destruction of a section of the ramparts next to the gate marked the end of papal temporal rule.

The Italian artillery, seeking to claim Rome for the Kingdom of Italy and thus add the ultimate missing piece to unite the country after the long and bloody war of independence, succeeded, after several hours of fire, in forcing the pope's supporters to retreat. Breaching the ramparts at the place that has passed into posterity as Breccia di Porta Pia, the Italian soldiers entered the city, cheered on by the jubilant residents.

It was Emperor Aurelian who had the walls that bear his name constructed between AD 270 and AD 273, to defend the capital of the empire against barbarian attack. Some 19 kilometres long, the walls have been restored several times, both in antiquity and in more recent times, and are still in good repair today over almost two-thirds of their original circuit.

A DEVIL WITH THE FEATURES OF A FUTURE POPE!
In the church of Santa Maria della Concezione dei Cappuccini (Our Lady of the Conception of the Capuchins) on Via Veneto, the first altar to the right holds a fine painting by Guido Reni, depicting the Archangel Michael casting down a

devil. This work was, however, not to everybody's taste: Cardinal Giovanni Battista Pamphili, the future Pope Innocent X, complained bitterly about the incredible likeness between the devil's features and his own. Reni changed nothing in his painting, for the cardinal had not shown himself to be particularly virtuous. Among other exploits, he is said to have been the lover of his sister-in-law Olimpia, who obtained from him the concession of running the Roman brothels, as the audio guide to the museum of Palazzo Doria Pamphili explains.

IPOGEO DI VIA LIVENZA

Via Livenza
• Visits on request, by telephoning the Cultural Heritage department of the Municipality of Rome (*Sovraintendenza Comunale ai Beni Culturali*) at 06 0608, alternatively through cultural associations such as *Roma Sotterranea* (www.romasotterranea.it).

A 4th-century AD hypogeum above a garage

I n 1923, during construction work on a private residence between Via Livenza and Via Po, about 250 metres from the Aurelian Wall, an underground structure dating from the second half of the 4th century AD was discovered but then partially destroyed. The preserved section contains a number of elements of great interest.

Access is by a door located along an access ramp to a private garage. Nine metres below, at the foot of the stairway, is an irregularly shaped chamber. One of the walls is particularly remarkable: an arch outlined by marble parapets encloses a deep rectangular bath, lined with waterproof concrete, at the bottom of which can be seen brick paving. Four steep and uneven steps lead to this bath, fitted with a system for supplying water. It cascaded down a terracotta pipe before flowing out through an opening with a valve connected to a drainage channel carved from the rock.

This hypogeum is lavishly decorated. In the centre of the rear wall above the bath there is a niche, the upper part of which is shaped like a fountain: the water runs down over a vase with two little birds perched on its rim. Just beside this niche, on the left, is a representation of Diana crowned with laurel leaves. The goddess is extracting an arrow from her quiver with her right hand, while holding the bow in her left. Two deer in flight can be seen. To the right of the niche is a nymph caressing the muzzle of a fawn. The side walls are tessellated with fused glass mosaics. Maritime scenes complete with *putti* add the finishing touches to this rich decorative art.

The monument is located in the heart of the Salario necropolis. Although almost all the structures excavated in the area are funerary monuments, the function of this one remains a mystery. Its basilical form, and especially the presence of the bath, suggests that it may originally have been a Christian baptismal hall.

Recently, other researchers have suggested that the hypogeum was a hideaway for practising magic, or perhaps a temple linked to a water cult, unless it was simply a nymphaeum or a fountain built to protect a natural underground spring.

HOUSE OF OWLS

Villa Torlonia, 70 Via Nomentana
• Tel: 06 44250072
• Bus: 36, 84, 60, 90, 140
• Opening times: Tuesday to Sunday, from April to September 9am - 7pm and from October to March 9am - 5pm. Closed 1 January, 1 May, 15 August, and 25 December
• Admission: €2.60; concessions €1.60

A fairytale house

Hidden behind an artificial hill in Torlonia park, the astonishing Casina delle Civette (House of Owls) intrigues the few visitors who happen upon it.

Once known as a "Swiss lodge", this curious fairytale house built by the architect Giusepe Jappelli in 1840, was enlarged and reorganised at the beginning of the last century. It was known as Villaggio Medievale (Medieval Village) after the first phase of restoration before taking its current name after the introduction of Liberty-style elements.

This bizarre construction, which was the residence of the Torlonias who owned the whole park from 1797 to 1939, was rented by Mussolini from 1925 to 1943 and it was then abandoned and ransacked for decades.

Today it is a singular yet harmonious superimposition of styles that after careful restoration has become a small museum of stained-glass windows, unique of its kind for the city of Rome, which has few remaining examples of the style of this period.

Apart from the large amount of wall, stucco and ceramic decorations and *boiseries*, the house has amazing polychrome stained-glass windows. They were designed by various artists at that time and made by Picchiarini, a master in this old art which came back into fashion at the beginning of the 20th century. Apart from the stained-glass windows commissioned by Giovanni Torlonia for the house, the small museum also exhibits other stained-glass windows and sketches from the artists' heirs and the Picchiarini records.

It is also worthwhile visiting the nearby Casino dei Principi (House of Princes), a building in the complex that was reopened as a museum after lengthy restoration work. Canova's sculptures, the busts and the room that was rebuilt by Giovanni Torlonia all illustrate the family's lifestyle at the time and the importance of the collection.

MUSSOLINI'S BUNKERS AT VILLA TORLONIA ❹

Villa Torlonia
70 Via Nomentana
• Visits on reservation only: Sovraintendenza Comunale (town planning services)
• Tel.: 06 0608

> *Three secret bunkers for Il Duce*

Villa Torlonia, the residence of Benito Mussolini from 1925 to 1943, dates from the 19th century. It is fitted with three bunkers, the construction of which first required the modification of a double cellar under the Fucino Basin (former lake bed where the villa is sited), fixing armour-plated doors, anti-gas filters, a bathroom and electricity. Even though it was only a short distance from Casino Nobile (the building where Mussolini and his family lived), this bunker was not a secure shelter in emergencies, because you had to cross open ground to reach it.

So it was decided to build a new shelter in the basement of Casino Nobile, where the villa kitchens were located. The ceiling was reinforced with a concrete framework and the living space fitted with two entrances and with sleeping compartments, which themselves had double gas-proof doors with peepholes.

This second solution was unlikely to have satisfied Il Duce, because a third bunker was built, a veritable air-raid shelter, linked by a tunnel to the basements of the villa. Consisting of two semi-circular galleries each about 10 metres long, laid out in the form of a cross with a reinforced concrete framework some 4 metres thick, it had two emergency exits that led directly into the park. This third shelter was never completed and the doors were not even fitted: on 25 July 1943, Mussolini was dismissed from office by the Fascist Grand Council, which had him arrested and replaced by General Badoglio.

HIDDEN SEPULCHRES

In one of the two sleeping compartments of the second bunker, recent archaeological excavations have unearthed a series of sepulchres dating from the 2nd century AD. One of the walls has three columbarium niches containing funerary urns, and a number of bodies have been found buried lying in a prone position, a customary fate for those presumed guilty of an infamous act.

THE ETRUSCAN TOMB OF VILLA TORLONIA

70 Via Nomentana
• Enquiries to Sovraintendenza Comunale (town planning services)
• Tel.: 06 0608

*A fake
Etruscan
tomb*

I n 2004, during reconstruction work at the Casino Nobile of Villa Torlonia, a forgotten room was rediscovered: an underground circular space 6 metres in diameter with a lowered cupola, built in the manner of an Etruscan tomb, the shape and decoration of which are reminiscent of Etruscan and Corinthian pottery.

This discovery confirmed once again the eclecticism and unusual taste of the Torlonia family, one of the last great Roman patrons of the arts who organised digs in the 1840s, bringing to light a number of Etruscan tombs in their estates of Cerveteri and Vulci. This room was probably designed by the architect Giovan Battista Caretti. It does in fact appear in some of his drawings, but it was thought never to have been built. The wall incorporates twenty niches that would have held vases and, just above, a red band with spiralling plant motifs, within which is reproduced the silhouette of a crowned female form dressed in a peplos and holding a mirror, perhaps the embodiment of Prudence. The cupola, the three superimposed orders of which are separated by bands of floral decoration, is painted with wolves and boars, dogs and hares, deer, birds and panthers. These black and ochre figures stand out against a cream-coloured background. In the centre an oculus, now closed, would have illuminated the room.

A corridor, which led directly from the basement of the villa to this room, was

partitioned off when an anti-aircraft shelter was built (see Mussolini's bunkers, pp. 263 and 293), while a second corridor leading to the theatre was blocked by a rockfall. Questions remain as to the function of this room: secret passage, unexpected place to surprise guests, or even, bearing in mind the Masonic sympathies of Prince Alessandro Torlonia, site of secret meetings between "brothers".

PIRANDELLO'S HOUSE

13-15 Via Antonio Bosio
• Tel: 06 44291853
• Metro: B - Bologna
• Opening times: Tuesday to Friday 9am - 1pm

> *The final years of a great writer*

O utside the circles of students and the literati, few know that you can visit Luigi Pirandello's Roman residence. In the studio embellished with beautiful bay windows overlooking the garden, all the furniture is still in its original position: the writing desk and the two glass bookcases dating back to 1910, which were brought here from previous dwellings, the couch, the armchair, a second writing desk and the shelves which were later installed, the library with its 2,000 volumes belonging to the writer, his typewriter, the paintings, four of which are by his son Fausto, and numerous manuscripts. This studio-living room is where Pirandello wrote famous works such as *Pensaci Giacomino!* (Think About It, Giacomino!) and *Così è (se vi pare)* (So It Is [If You Think So]), and where he welcomed eminent friends such as Lucio d'Ambra and Silvio d'Amico. Much more sober and austere, on the other hand, is the bedroom where Pirandello slept and where he died and where his clothes, hats, walking stick and Accademico d'Italia uniform are still kept in the wardrobe.

This house is full of charm and memories and today is the headquarters of the Istituto di Studi Pirandelliani e Sul Teatro Italiano (Institute for the Study of Pirandello and Contemporary Italian Theatre). The aim of the institute, which was founded in 1962, is to promote the study of the life and works of Luigi Pirandello and contemporary theatre, to look after the studio, but above all to preserve and catalogue Pirandello's documents. The studio is open to the public.

LUIGI PIRANDELLO

The great writer and playwright Luigi Pirandello was born in Girgenti (now Agrigento) in 1867. Initially he studied in Sicily, then at Rome University, and he graduated from Bonn. In his novels, short stories and plays, he told of man's difficulty in finding reality beyond appearances and the scheme of things, and the drama of his incapacity to identify with his own nature. In 1934, two years before his death, he received the Nobel Prize for Literature. Some of his most famous works are *The Late Mattia Pascal*; *One, None and a Hundred Thousand* (1926); and the collection of *Short Stories for a Year*. In Italy and abroad, his greatest success was the theatre, with plays such as *Six Characters in Search of an Author*, *Sicilian Limes*, *Henry IV*, and *Così è (se vi pare)*, interpreted by the greatest theatre companies of their time. He died in Rome in 1936.

COPPEDÈ DISTRICT

- Entrance arch: crossroads between Viale Regina Margherita and Via Po
- Bus: 63, 86, 92, 630
- Tram: 3, 19

A bizarre district

Relatively unknown to Romans not living in this area, and even less so to tourists as it is away from the centre, the Quartiere Coppedè (Coppedè district) extends from Viale Regina Margherita to Via Tagliamento and it is the work of the Florentine architect of the same name: Gino Coppedè.

In 1917, the company that had acquired the 30,000 m² plot of land, with the plan to build a modern and elegant district destined for the middle class, entrusted Coppedè with the design and construction. Rarely has an architect had so much freedom in designing and completing an entire district. Coppedè, with his vast repertory of styles and using medieval, Florentine and mannerist elements, conceived a series of fantastic buildings. Balconies and

pinnacles, richly decorated balustrades and columns, outside walls frescoed with scenes celebrating Tuscan artists, the Fontana delle Rane (Frog Fountain), the three Villini delle Fate (fairy houses) that occupy the eastern side of Piazza Mincio, every detail of this area adds to the peculiar nature of the district.

GINO COPPEDÈ

Architect Gino Coppedè was born in Florence in 1866 and died in Rome in 1927. His extremely original and eclectic style, with its medieval, Renaissance and Liberty elements that blend to create architecture from a fairytale world, is found in all his buildings. His works include: the Mackenzie Castle (Genoa, 1890), the San Pierdarena pavilion (Milan, 1906), the Coppedè district (Rome, 1916-1926), the Tonietti Mausoleum on the island of Elba, Villa Merello (San Pantaleo in Liguria), Villa La Gaeta (San Abbondio on Lake Como) and fourteen buildings in Messina (Sicily). Most of the latter, such as those along Corso Garibaldi, are very dilapidated.

LA BOTTEGA DEL SOLDATINO

13 Via Lago di Lesina
- Tel: 06 86213452
- Bus: 63, 86, 92
- Opening times: 10am-1pm and 3:30pm-7:30pm

> *The oldest toy soldier manufacturer*

Toy soldier fans, collectors or simply all those who loved and owned toy soldiers in their childhood, should visit the shop-workshop of Luciano Antonini and discover the great family tradition.

The Antoninis are in fact the oldest toy soldier and military model manufacturers in Italy, and in Europe they are among those who have been making them longest. Even today, after almost a century, collectable toy soldiers are produced, hand-painted one by one, restored and sold in this small and charming shop. These soldiers are veritable miniature masterpieces.

The activity began in 1910 when Francesco Antonini at a very young age began to produce Prussian soldiers, British infantry, Hussars, cowboys, Indians and small leaden sailing ships, using aluminium moulds imported from Germany. These moulds are still preserved today in the workshop. In 1912, Francesco Antonini began to make his own moulds and figurines and to distribute them with the L.G.P. trademark (Laboratorio Giocattoli in Piombo – lead toy workshop). These bronze moulds were in two parts, which meant that fully round models could be made, not just semi-round models like the German ones.

The first series of toy soldiers – the Italian and Ottoman army in the Italo-Turkish war – were a great success with children at the time, as were all the others that followed, with up-to-date uniforms, in tune with those of the "real" army. The figurines of this period were real toys and only afterwards did they become collectors' items.

Luciano Antonini has worked with his father since he was a boy and has kept the business going by creating new series in the standard 54 mm size, replacing the stylised trotting horses with more realistic horses and introducing more modern machines. Since 1970, in cooperation with G. Del Vecchio, he has also been producing particularly realistic and detailed models in kits for enthusiasts who prefer to assemble and paint their figurines themselves.

MUSEO DI STORIA DELLA MEDICINA

34a Viale dell'Università
- Metro: Policlinico or Castro Pretorio
- Open Monday to Friday 9:30am-1:30pm and Tuesday and Thursday 2:30pm-5pm
- E-mail: museo.stomed@uniroma1.it • www.histmed.it
- Guided tours on reservation
- Tel.: 06 49914445

A trip back in time

Part of the Università degli Studi di Roma "La Sapienza", the remarkable though little-known Museum of the History of Medicine brings together charming reconstructions of historical settings with the educational interest of a modern museum. Most of the collections were amassed in 1938 by Adalberto Pazzini, founder of the museum and former professor at La Sapienza.

On the first floor, visitors will find a modern section with exhibitions of the history of medicine, from prehistoric times to today's technology. The antiquities section presents Egyptian, Greek and Roman medicine with educational aids such as plaster casts and reproductions of surgical instruments. The most interesting display concerns Etruscan medicine: you discover, for example, that the Etruscans had efficient techniques for replacing rotten teeth, but with animal rather than human teeth as it was forbidden to plunder the dead. You can also see the bronze reproduction of a sheep's liver dating from the 3rd to 2nd centuries BC, subdivided into zones corresponding to parts of the heavens. Animal organs were, in fact, used by haruspices (seers) to foretell the future.

The medieval section throws light on monastic medicine and the re-establishment of scientific medicine in the West based on the Arab tradition.

In the modern section, the accent is on the Italian contribution to medicine from the late Middle Ages to the Renaissance. In 1316, it was the Italian physician and anatomist Mondino De' Luzzi who carried out the first dissection at a University of Bologna public lecture. There is a fine model of the first anatomy theatre built at the University of Padua, thanks to the determination

of Girolamo Fabrici (Fabricius ab Acquapendente), the Italian surgeon who discovered the valves of the veins.

The reconstructions in the basement offer a double trip back in time. There is an alchemist's laboratory, a Renaissance medical lecture hall, a 17th-century apothecary's shop, and more. Pazzini also collected pottery jars from Italian and French pharmacies of the 17th and 18th centuries.

THE FOUNDATION OF THE CERERE PASTA FACTORY

⑩

Via degli Ausoni, 7
• www.pastificiocerere.com • Email: info@pastificiocerere.it
• Tel.: 06 454 22 960
• Open Monday to Friday 3pm-7pm

An artist factory

Aptly dedicated to Ceres, Roman goddess of the harvest or agriculture, the Cerere semolina and pasta factory was founded in 1905. The company headquarters are located in a beautiful ensemble of courtyards and buildings overlooking Via Tiburtina, Via degli Ausoni and Piazza dei Sanniti in the San Lorenzo district.

The oldest building in the neighbourhood, today it is one of the finest examples of an industrial reconversion. After falling into disuse in 1960, the factory came back to life when a group of artists decided to settle there in the late 1970s and early 1980s.

These past years, a group of young painters, photographers and sculptors has come to join the original group of artists historically known as the Gruppo di San Lorenzo. A non-profit foundation was also created at the behest of its president, Flavio Misciattelli.

The premises of the old factory have been transformed into superb lofts where the artists have set up their studios. Countless projects are brought to life here, beginning with temporary exhibitions and the creation of a permanent collection dedicated to the historic artists. The Foundation has given art lovers access to the cultural heritage and creative initiatives that have characterised this legendary site for thirty years. Located at the heart of the former factory, the head office is an open space measuring nearly 200 m² in what was once the corn loft. The Foundation intends to use the space to promote both young and more well-established artists by organising one- to three-month-long temporary exhibitions as part of a year-long programme. You can consult the programme at the Foundation's headquarters.

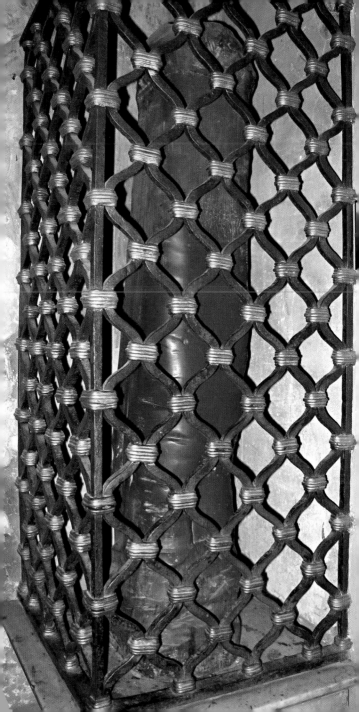

THE DUST OF THE PILLAR OF SANTA BIBIANA ⑪

Church of Santa Bibiana
154 Via G. Giolitti
• Opening hours: 7:30am-11am and 4:30pm-7:30pm
• Transport: Trams 5 or 14; Metro A or B – Termini

> **A potion made from the blood of a martyr**

L ocated just a short distance from the Termini train station and squeezed between the tracks of old and new railway lines, this small church goes unnoticed due to its unfortunate position, hidden by the train pylons, by its own enclosure, and by trees. To find the entrance, you have to cross the old tracks and a street that is difficult for pedestrians to access.

It is, in fact, an old basilica dedicated to Bibiana, a legendary 4th-century martyr. It was built in the 5th century at the behest of Pope Simplicius over the remains of thousands of martyrs. Reconstructed for the first time by Pope Honorius III in 1224, it was reconstructed a second time by Pope Urban VIII in 1626, with numerous interventions by Bernini, who gave it a new façade with an atrium and a loggia that were later closed. Bernini redesigned the apse, adding two chapels to the lateral naves at the back, where the altar paintings depicting Defrosa di Pietro da Cortona and Demetria di Agostino Ciampelli (Bibiana's mother and sister respectively, both martyrs) can be seen. He also renovated the main chapel, inserting a statue of Bibiana in a niche.

Under the main altar, a precious alabaster jar contains the remains of Bibiana, Demetria and Defrosa. The trunk of the pillar to which Bibiana was tied and flogged to death is kept in the left-hand nave.

It is worn down by the hands of all those who for centuries have scraped up the dust. By dissolving this dust in water from the well in the nearby kitchen garden, and mixing it with the grass growing on the spot where the martyr's blood flowed, believers try to obtain a potion with miraculous powers.

KITCHEN GARDEN OF SANTA CROCE IN GERUSALEMME

⑫

9/A Piazza di Santa Croce in Gerusalemme
• Tel: 06 7014796
• Bus: 571, 649; Tram: 3
• Open Wednesdays 9:45am – 1pm and 2:30pm – 5pm or by prior reservation

> *A monastic garden in the city centre*

Hidden behind a gate, on the grounds of the church of Santa Croce in Gerusalemme (Holy Cross of Jerusalem), lies the kitchen garden of the Cistercian monks who live in the adjacent monastery. A surprising piece of countryside, this garden has been restored and can be visited.

The garden has existed for 500 years and has always been cultivated by monks, who would eat the crops they grew. Although in recent times the garden had become seriously run down, the monks and the landscape gardener Paolo Pejrone worked together to bring it back to its original beauty. By removing the unhealthy trees, the cabins and the corrugated iron roofs, the kitchen garden has recovered its harmonious form. Its serene and almost magical atmosphere affects all those who visit it.

The plot, which occupies 8,000 m² behind its high walls, is divided into

four sectors with paths laid out in cruciform shape, among which you can stroll in the shade of pergolas covered with vines and white roses, while admiring the flower and strawberry beds. Where the paths cross is a large basin for watering the plants. The monks grow artichokes, organic lettuces, broad beans and aromatic herbs with which they produce *crocino*, an after-dinner drink invented by Brother Gilberto, a monk who was particularly devoted to the vegetable garden.

THE INRI INSCRIPTION AT SANTA CROCE IN GERUSALEMME ⓭

Chapel of Relics and Sanctuary of the Cross
Piazza di Santa Croce in Gerusalemme, 9A
• Opening hours: daily 7am-1pm and 2pm-6:30pm
• www.basilicasantacroce.it
• Tel.: 06 70 14 769

> **Where is the True Cross of Christ?**

Among the main relics in the Basilica of Santa Croce in Gerusalemme (Holy Cross in Jerusalem) is that of the inscription on the cross on which Christ was crucified.

St John's Gospel is the only one that mentions this inscription. In his text, the words "Jesus of Nazareth the King of the Jews" are said to have been written in three languages: Hebrew, Greek and Latin. Note that, according to this same Gospel, the Jewish priests had asked Pilate that the inscription should instead read: "He said, I am King of the Jews", but Pilate refused.

The tradition is that a fragment of the cross bearing this inscription was brought back from the Holy Land by Helena, mother of Constantine, the first Roman emperor to convert to Christianity and founder of Constantinople, the city named after him.

According to Saint Ambrose, Bishop of Milan (died 397), Helena discovered the True Cross of Christ in 325, distinguishing it from the two other crucifixes thanks to the famous inscription. She then brought the fragment back to Rome, for her palace at Sessoriano, within which the Basilica of Santa Croce in Gerusalemme was built. Later, similar relics cropped up elsewhere (see pages 138-139), until several crosses and inscriptions were competing with each other. Another INRI inscription was reported in Jerusalem at the end of the 4th century, but this one had a different wording: *Hic est Rex Iudaeorum* (This is the King of the Jews). A third inscription came to light in Paris in the 13th century and a fourth was displayed in the cathedral of Toulouse.

The inscription of Santa Croce in Gerusalemme was rediscovered in 1492, concealed behind a stone in the wall, in a lead box with the seal of Pope Lucius II (1144-1145). In 2001, two scientists, Francesco Bella and Carlo Azzi, analysed it by carbon-14 dating and found that it originated around 1020.

KING OF THE JEWS: A TERM LOADED WITH MEANING?

For some experts, such as M. Baigent, R. Leigh and H. Lincoln,* the term "King of the Jews" is not just idle talk. At the time of Christ, Palestine was occupied by the Romans and this state of affairs was intolerable to many Jews. In addition to his great spiritual message, which nobody denies, Jesus, as a direct descendant of David and Solomon, would in fact have had a claim to the title of King of the Jews, with a mission to liberate his people from the Roman yoke. This would also help to explain why Jesus, representing a major political threat to Rome, was sentenced to be crucified.

* See *The Holy Blood and the Holy Grail* and *The Messianic Legacy*, both published by Dell US and Arrow UK.

CAN THE TRUE CROSS BE TRACED BACK TO ADAM, SOLOMON AND THE QUEEN OF SHEBA?

According to the *Legenda aurea* (*Golden Legend*) by Jacobus de Voragine (1228-1298), Adam in his great age asked his son Seth to procure oil from the Archangel Michael to anoint him before he died. The archangel refused but instead gave him a small branch from the Tree of [Knowledge of] Good and Evil with the command to place it in Adam's mouth at the moment of his burial. This small branch would then grow from Adam's body into a great tree that would save him from his sins, ensuring his salvation.

Much later, when King Solomon was having the Temple of Jerusalem built, this tree was cut down to be used in the construction, but it so happened that the beam kept changing size and was either too short or too long for its intended use. The workmen got rid of it by casting it into the River Siloe to use as a footbridge.

The Queen of Sheba, who had journeyed to visit Solomon, had a premonition as soon as she stepped on the bridge: this beam of wood will one day be used for the crucifixion of Christ and the reign of the Jews will come to an end. In order to avoid this tragic fate, King Solomon had the beam taken away and buried. At the time of Jesus' trial, however, the beam sprang miraculously from the soil and was ultimately used for the cross on which he was crucified. In order to avoid crosses becoming cult objects, they were buried and forgotten until the Roman Emperor Constantine, while fighting his rival Maxentius, had a vision of an illuminated cross on which was inscribed: *"in hoc signo vinces"* ["In this sign, conquer"]. His army having won the decisive battle of the Milvian Bridge by following the sign of the cross, Constantine wished to recover the Cross of Christ and sent his mother Helena to Jerusalem to look for it.

After torturing a Jew who knew the burial site of the three crosses [Jesus and the two thieves] for seven days, Helena rediscovered them. A miraculous event then revealed which of the three was the True Cross: a young man who had just died was instantly revived when his lifeless body touched the wood of the Cross of Christ.

Part of the Cross was retained in Jerusalem while another fragment was taken to Constantinople, the new imperial capital.

THE BAKER'S TOMB

Piazza Maggiore

> **An imperial tomb for a simple baker**

Virtually an imperial monument, the monument to Marco Virgilio Eurisace is just the tomb of an ordinary baker. It was rediscovered in the late 19th century when Pope Gregory XVI demolished the defensive towers that Honorius had built beside the Porta Maggiore in 1838, in order to restore the site to the aspect it enjoyed in the Aurelian era. Constructed from concrete and travertine in 30 BC, the monument curiously resembles the patrician tombs of the Appian Way.

As the inscription points out: *Est hoc monimentum Marcei Vergilei Eurysacis pistoris, redemptoris, apparet* (This is the tomb of Marcus Vergilius Eurysaces, baker, contractor, provisioning breadmaker). The man, who was a subordinate (*apparitore*) to a high-ranking figure, was probably an emancipated slave who worked for the state.

On the tomb are a number of symbols of the baker's trade. The tomb itself is shaped like the vessel in which he would have kneaded the bread. It is decorated with numerous bas-reliefs representing the utensils used to make bread, as well as the production process itself: weighing the wheat, sifting the flour, preparing the dough, placing the bread in the oven …

The urn in which the ashes of his wife Atinia are preserved, now in the Museo delle Terme in Rome, was made in the form of a dough trough. Finally, the bas-relief depicting two spouses at the Capitoline Museums probably comes from another, now ruined, section of this monument.

The Museo della Civiltà Romana (Museum of Roman Civilisation), in the EUR district, holds a miniature reproduction of the tomb.

The Porta Maggiore was so named to indicate to pilgrims the route that led to the church of Santa Maria Maggiore.

MAGISTRI

Via Ardeatina km 23,200
• Tel.: 067887472

> **Buy
> the headlamp
> of a tank**

Going along Via del Mandrione towards the centre, a gateway suddenly breaks the high wall on the right-hand side and leads to one of the few used-technology shops – only about a dozen similar places remain in all of Europe.

The last remaining survivor from the dynasty of "surplus" traders, who in the early 1960s spilled over from the stalls in Porta Portese, Rome's flea market, Magistri is an amazing shop. In this huge hall and the even bigger outdoor space, in an atmosphere straight out of "Blade Runner", you can find almost everything. D.I.Y. electronics enthusiasts will be in their true realm here and for a modest sum can bring home military radio transmitters that still work, electronic components of every type, instruments, transistors, valves, transformers and integrated circuits.

The Italian tradition of dealing in spare parts for electronic appliances, fine mechanics or optics of military origin began around the end of the Second World War in the city of Naples, which had only just been freed by the Allies. It became a flourishing economic activity.

But even browsers can appreciate the great bowls of multi-coloured dismantled electronic devices, which seem like piles of sweets or gems and that a young Brazilian architect actually uses to make jewellery. They can also look over, from bottom to top, the ominous silhouette of a radar support that rises above a mound of vacuum pumps three floors high, or even an old fighter plane, a locomotive, or armoured first-aid kits - army surplus piled high as trailers.

Someone with a little imagination can bring home a gas mask for modern day miasmas, or a very efficient headlamp from an armoured car to light a terrace or a garden with a ray of light that illuminates for over one kilometre. They can even purchase nocturnal binoculars to spy at night on their neighbours, or an armoured generator, to cope with possible major power cuts.

The owners and salespeople move around among the mazes of the place like guardians of this post-modern museum of white elephants. They are passionate about their job and will spend time helping customers with their purchases or simply satisfying their curiosity. Among the customers there are cinema people, who have come to rent military telephones from the Second World War for a film setting, or even researchers hunting for measuring equipment and instruments that are normally extremely expensive.

MUSEO DELLA MEMORIA GIOCOSA

24-26 Via Vincenzo Coronelli
- Tel: 06 24407777
- Bus: 105, 157, 553, 545
- Tram: 5, 14, 19
- Opening times: Wednesday to Friday 3pm - 7pm, Saturday to Sunday 10am - 12pm and 3pm - 7pm
- Admission free

> **Toys in their thousands**

The Museum of Childhood Memories (Museo della Memoria Giocosa) opened in 1979 thanks to the collection that Lisa and Franco Palmieri inherited from Fritz Billig, an Austrian who took refuge in New York following the arrival of Nazism. He managed to take his childhood toys with him, which included wind-up toys and cars by Lehman and Tippco, Jewish companies requisitioned by Hitler's Germany.

Children from all over Europe, regardless of their culture, race or religion, played with these toys. For Billig, they became the symbol of an ideal world where everyone would be equal. This notion encouraged him to continue collecting toys for the rest of his life. Today his collection is exhibited in this museum, a space of about 300 m² in the Pigneto-Prenestino-Labicano district.

The collection comprises European, American and Asian toys and games made between 1920 and 1960. The museum also has a 60-seat theatre, Albero delle Favole (The Story Tree), where children's shows are organised. There is also a bar, a thematic library, catalogues, posters, brochures and objects linked to the world of toys as well as a very interesting collection of illustrative and advertising material on cars.

This remarkable museum, the only one of its kind in Italy, also contains a large-scale model railway layout dating from 1937.

THE *SALVATOR MUNDI* BY BERNINI

Basilica of San Sebastiano fuori le mura
136 Via Appia Antica
• Bus: 218; or 5 km on foot from Circo Massimo
• Tel: 06 78 87 035
• Open daily 8am - 7pm

> *Bernini's last masterpiece found!*

The basilica of San Sebastiano fuori le mura (Saint Sebastian outside the walls) flanks the celebrated Appian Way, the *regina viarum* ("queen of roads"). In 2001, Bernini's last masterpiece, still largely unknown to the general public, was found in the adjoining convent.

To reach the basilica, you can avoid the traffic by following the route of the catacombs of Saint Calixtus, departing from the church known as *Domine Quo Vadis* and emerging near the basilica. Strangely enough, you will pass sheep grazing along the roadside.

A church was first built here in the 4th century on the site of the catacombs of Saint Sebastian. It was rebuilt by Pope Nicholas I (858-867), but we owe the present edifice to Cardinal Scipion Borghese (1576-1633) who had it built at the beginning of the 17th century. The façade dates from the 18th century.

In August 2001, through a series of coincidences, art historians identified a statue by Bernini in a small niche at the entrance to the convent of Saint Sebastian. The work, which had been sought for a long time, and allegedly found several times since 1972, had disappeared at the end of the 17th century.

The bust now stands beside the Relics Chapel. The finesse of the marble sculpture, and the gesture of the hand raised in blessing, is proof enough that we are in the presence of work by the great master of Baroque sculpture, Gian Lorenzo Bernini (1598-1680). The *Salvator Mundi* is a marble bust of Christ that is considered to be his last masterpiece, sculpted in 1679. Bernini's son, Pier Filippo, wrote in his 1680 biography of his father that the latter had "worked in marble until his 81st year, which he finished with a Saviour out of his devotion".

In the Relics Chapel is a stone bearing the imprint of the foot of Christ at the moment when he appeared to Saint Peter. Tradition has it that, fleeing Rome to avoid persecution, Peter met the risen Jesus along the Appian Way and asked him: "*Quo vadis, Domine?*" ("Where are you going, Lord?"). Jesus answered: "*Eo Romam iterum crucifigi.*" ("I am going to Rome to be crucified again.") This meeting convinced Peter to retrace his steps and face martyrdom in Rome.

The Relics Chapel also contains one of the arrows that struck Saint Sebastian during his martyrdom. Directly opposite is a beautiful sculpture of the saint by Antonio Giorgetti, one of Bernini's pupils.

AIR-RAID SHELTER IN THE EUR DISTRICT

8 Piazzale K. Adenauer
• Individual tours Saturdays and Sundays.
• Groups by appointment with Suerte s.r.l. Tel: 06 44340160;
Mobile: 333.5085905 www.suerteitinerarte.it

> *Mussolini's bunker ...*

The EUR district lies on the south side of Rome, along the intended route of the subway planned during the Fascist period to link the central government buildings on the Capitoline hill with the seashore. The entire zone was to be the site of the 1942 World's Fair (Esposizione Universale di Roma, hence the acronym EUR, or E42), which was cancelled because of the Second World War.

The construction of some of the buildings was begun in 1938, but many were left unfinished until after 1951, following radical changes to the initial project. The zone was then relaunched to host a number of competitions during the 1960 Olympics.

When the administrative centre of Palazzo degli Uffici was built, an air-raid shelter was added in the sub-basement which, according to the designers, could hold as many as 300 people. The pre-war international political climate was so tense that such a structure did seem necessary.

A gap some two metres wide isolates the bunker from the rest of the building. The entire construction consisted of reinforced concrete in order to deaden the shockwaves from bombardments.

Even though it has never been used, this bunker is fitted with gas-proof double doors with peepholes, as well as ventilation and air-filtration systems. It is equipped with remarkable electrical installations powered by two specially adapted bicycles. There were also lavatories and a kitchen. Some of the original notices with instructions for the occupants can still be seen.

You can also visit another air-raid shelter in Villa Torlonia, which was the private residence of Benito Mussolini from 1925. Two underground bunkers – one gas-proof and the other bomb-proof – were also added in the basement (see page 263).

THE THREE COLUMBARIA OF VIGNA CODINI AND THE TOMB OF POMPONIUS HYLAS ⓳

Columbaria of Vigna Codini: 14 Via di Porta Latina, on private property
Tomb of Pomponius Hylas: 10 Via di Porta Latina, in Scipion park
Visits: • Columbaria of Vigna Codini: contact any of the numerous cultural
associations (e.g. *Roma Sotterranea*, www.romasotterranea.it).
• Tomb of Pomponius Hylas: on request by telephoning the Cultural
Heritage department of the Municipality of Rome (*Sovraintendenza
Comunale ai Beni Culturali*) at 06 0608, alternatively through cultural
associations such as *Roma Sotterranea* (www.romasotterranea.it)

> *Some
> of the most
> fascinating
> tombs in Rome*

O n leaving Rome by the Porta Latina, after a short distance you will notice a gateway on the left leading to private villas. In this intimate environment and in the adjoining public park some of the city's most fascinating tombs can be found.

The columbaria of Vigna Codini are imposing funerary monuments, each of which once held hundreds of tombs. The cinerary urns of members of corporations or associations were laid to rest there. Each niche could hold several urns and was marked with a plaque bearing the name and sometimes even the sculpted portrait of the deceased. The first columbarium indicated, intended for the freed slaves of the emperors Tiberius and Claudius, is the most majestic: in the centre of a rectangular space of around 40 m² an enormous pillar supports the lattice vaults. Dozens of niches have been carved within this pillar.

The second columbarium, some 7 metres deep and rectangular in plan, includes the tombs of members of a college of musicians and those of a flower merchants' guild. In certain places, you can still see sections of wall paintings in particularly bright colours.

Designed in a U-shape, the third columbarium was occupied by the tombs of slaves of the Julian-Claudian dynasty. The vault is richly decorated and there is a small adjoining chamber (called the *ustrinum*) where bodies were cremated, a rather unusual arrangement for a building which, like the preceding two, was intended to receive the bodies of the lower classes.

The tomb of Pomponius Hylas, reached through the adjoining public gardens, belonged to a wealthy family that could afford its own underground sepulchre. It dates from the first half of the 1st century AD. Built along the same lines as a small columbarium, it is richly decorated with bas-reliefs and polychrome stucco-work, as well as paintings and mosaics. This tomb, although rather cramped, is almost intact (with the exception of a few missing motifs) and all the more disconcerting because it gives the impression of having remained unchanged for over two millennia.

THE CISTERN OF VIA CRISTOFORO COLOMBO ⓴

Via Cristoforo Colombo, level with No. 142 (Ostiense)
• Visits on request, by telephoning the Cultural Heritage department of
the Municipality of Rome (*Sovraintendenza Comunale ai Beni Culturali*)
at 06 0608, alternatively through cultural associations such as *Roma
Sotterranea* (www.romasotterranea.it)

> *The remains
> of an ancient
> water tank*

The two circular buildings adjoining Via Cristoforo Colombo at the junction of Circonvallazione Ostiense and Piazza dei Navigatori are actually the remains of a water tank.

A farmhouse concealed their presence until it was demolished at the end of the 1930s to make way for the construction of the former Via Imperiale, a highway that linked the city to the coast.

The larger of the two buildings dates back to the first half of the 2nd century AD and was intended to supply agricultural needs in the area. It measures some 15 metres in diameter and apparently was used as a cistern, as borne out by the traces of cement on the walls and a system of pipes that could empty the cistern for maintenance, although it has not yet been established how water was brought in or where it came from. Inside are two concentric rings of corridors, the first ring consisting of ten barrel-vaulted sections separated by archways, while the second forms a single circular room. From there, a corridor leads to a central chamber that is 3 metres in diameter. All these chambers are in very poor condition, the structure having been converted and redeveloped more than once.

The second building, of more recent date, could not have held water due to the thinness of its walls, but we still do not know what it was used for.

Although this neighbourhood was a suburb (*suburbio*) on the outskirts of the city, it would have been well connected to the heart of Rome by the Appian Way only a few hundred metres away, at least, that is, until the construction of the Aurelian Wall (AD 271-275).

JEWISH CATACOMBS OF VIGNA RANDANINI ㉑

4 Via Appia Pignatelli, in the grounds of a private residence (Appia Antica)
• Visits on request, through the cultural association *Roma Sotterranea*
(www.romasotterranea.it).

> **The only
> Jewish
> catacombs
> in Rome open
> to the public**

Discovered around 1859, the Jewish catacombs of Vigna Randanini, on the Appia Pignatelli road, date from the 3rd century AD and are the only catacombs of their kind in Rome that can be visited. Not all these galleries, extending over a surface of almost 720 m² at a depth of some 10 metres, are accessible.

A small building on the surface houses an entry to the catacombs. It is thought that during the original construction phase (first half of the 2nd century AD), they consisted simply of a square chamber characterised by two exedras and a niche. The second phase (3rd-4th centuries) was notable for the general reorganization of the whole structure, which nevertheless spared the two exedras. It was probably during this phase that the black and white mosaic paving that can still be seen today was installed.

On entering the galleries, it is immediately clear that most of the tombs are in the form of niches, arches, or small funerary chambers.

In a section further away from the entrance are a great number of kokhim (hollowed-out tombs typical of Jewish culture, of which there are no other examples in Rome). Three of the funerary chambers are decorated with paintings: the first consists of frescoes with simple geometric motifs, coloured red on a white background; the second, preceded by a vestibule rendered in white, is embellished in the four corners with date palms.

But it is in the galleries on the lower level where the rooms with the most interesting frescoes are to be found, including a double chamber with geometrical decorations and divisions. The various images are shown inside a honeycomb of cells. The central ceiling motif of the first chamber is a Winged Victory surrounded by peacocks, birds and baskets of fruit, in the act of crowning a naked young man. In the second chamber, the central figure of the vault is an allegory of Fortune with a horn of abundance in her hand. The border is decorated with fish and ducks interspersed with baskets of fruit. The four seasons are represented in the corners of the chamber.

The rear wall, today badly damaged, depicted a man standing between two horses.

The catacombs were also covered with a number of Latin and Greek inscriptions, most of which are now illegible.

THE CHURCH OF TOR TRE TESTE

Via Francesco Tovaglieri
• Bus: 556
• Opening times: 7:30am-12:30pm and 3:30pm-7:30pm

Very modern art in Rome

The church of Dives in Misericordia (the Church of God Our Merciful Father) in the Roman district of the Tor Tre Teste is worth visiting for many reasons. This church was the first project in Rome by Richard Meier, an American architect of international renown. One of the very few examples of contemporary art applied to a religious building, this church is important above all for the choice of location, which expresses an attempt to redevelop the outskirts of Rome.

The famous architect, who also designed buildings such as the Getty Center in Los Angeles, the High Museum in Atlanta, the Barcelona Museum of Contemporary Art and the Canal Plus Television Headquarters in Paris, won the international competition organised by the Vatican in 1996 with his daring ideas for this project.

As part of an overall plan to build 50 new churches in Rome for the Jubilee, the church, begun in 1998, was completed too late for the year 2000, but in time to celebrate the 25 years of Pope John Paul II's pontificate. Its most characteristic elements are the three giant cement sails of increasing size, each weighing 12 tons, giving the building the shape of a large sailboat.

They symbolically represent the Church's entry into the third millennium.

Meier, known as the architect of light, wanted to express beauty and spirituality. He has succeeded in giving this place a mystical atmosphere, thanks to the light that floods the whole building, the shapes, the transparency of the glass, the snow-white marbles, the simple interior and the sense of movement given to the sails.

ROME IN THE ERA OF CONTEMPORARY ART

Rome is not entirely stuck in its own past, as recent and up-coming architectural creations illustrate. What makes it different is that, Rome being what it is, the city has only called on the greatest contemporary architects.

Ara Pacis Museum – Richard Meier
Auditorium – Renzo Piano
MAXXI (National Museum of XXI Century Arts) – Zaha Hadid
MACRO – Odile Decq
Congress Centre – EUR – Massimiliano Fuksas

MUSEUM OF PERIOD COACHES

693 Via Millevoi
• Tel: 06 51958112 • Bus: 766
• Opening times: Tuesday to Friday 10am-1pm and 3:30pm-7pm, Saturday and Sunday 9:30am-1:30pm and 3:30pm-7:30pm
• Admission: €5.16 full price, €3.62 concessions

Vehicles of yesteryear

In this recently opened museum, an exceptional collection of period carriages and characteristic coaches is exhibited. They have been acquired over a period of forty years by their passionate owner. The collection is made up of 293 models, half of which are exhibited. Most of them have been restored and are in perfect working order. These splendid coaches occupy an exhibition space of 3,000 m², offering a striking overall view assembled here, but they also constitute a precious cultural heritage, as each one of them testifies to a historic and social reality. Apart from the coaches, over one hundred pieces including saddles and trappings are also exhibited. The museum is in the Ardeatina area, close to the catacombs of San Callistus and to the Archaeological Park of Appia Antica. The exhibition is managed by a cultural non-profit-making association. Among the exhibits are the hackney coach that belonged to Anna Magnani, which she used to move around the city during the war, Ben Hur's chariot, the pram given to Princess Sissi of Austria-Hungary when she was small and the horse-drawn carriage used by John Wayne in *The Quiet Man*. There are also carriages from the 18th and 19th centuries, firemen's coaches, American stagecoaches, mail wagons and seven monumental carriages decorated with frescoes of the 19th century belonging to the city of Rome.

SIGHTS NEARBY

Mausoleo di Monte del Grano

Piazza dei Tribuni (Via Tuscolana - Quadraro)
• Visits on request, by contacting cultural associations such as *Roma Sotterranea* (www.romasotterranea.it)

The large buildings of the working-class district of Quadraro screen an imposing tomb, the third largest in Rome, surpassed only by the mausoleums of Hadrian and Augustus. This mausoleum was nicknamed "Monte del Grano" because of its shape, reminiscent of an upturned ear of wheat, after the blocks of travertine that had originally covered it had been removed for other uses. The construction, 12 metres high, with a circumference of 140 metres, now looks like a small overgrown hill. Access is by a 20 metre corridor opening onto a circular enclosure with brick-lined walls, about 10 metres in diameter. In the past, this enclosure was divided into two floors and two shafts provided light and ventilation. In 1582 a large sarcophagus, now in the Capitoline Museums, was found inside, which was thought to feature the Emperor Severus Alexander (AD 222-235). In fact, the markings on some of the bricks show that the structure had been built well before then, during the reign of the Emperor Hadrian (around AD 150). In any case, such an important monument could certainly only have been intended for a leading representative of the imperial family or for a senator.

THE CORVIALE

Via Poggio Verde
• Bus: 701, 771, 773, 785, 786

> A
> **building
> one kilometre
> long**

The Nuovo Corviale is a complex built in the 1970s in the south-west of the city and to the right of Via Portuense in the direction of Fiumicino. This very peculiar structure, which is about one kilometre long, is nine storeys high, and has two more floors of cellars and a basement. It houses 1,202 apartments in five blocks, a lower parallel building and another one built across it. A pedestrian street with some shops also crosses it.

The original design, which calls to mind the theories of the famous architect Le Corbusier, was given to a team of twenty-three designers headed by the architect Mario Fiorentino. Its most revolutionary aspect is the communal areas: offices, meeting halls, common rooms, library, art school, open-air theatres, indoor gymnasium, crèches, schools, pharmacy, indoor market, restaurant, shops, large green spaces and craft workshops.

All of these spaces were planned on a large scale in order to serve the surrounding quarter, as well as the twenty new buildings planned for the area that would welcome an additional 1,500 inhabitants.

Building began in 1975 and the first apartments were allocated in 1982. From 1983, over 700 families with urgent housing needs occupied the housing provided and, above all, the community areas. Another 150 settled in tents in the square at the foot of the complex for a year and a half. The Nuovo Corviale, therefore, has never fully performed the role for which it was created.

ALFONSO TOZZI'S COLLECTION

27 Via Pescaglia
- Tel: 06 55285165
- Bus: 780, 781
- Opening times: prior reservation required

> *27,000 razor blades*

Alfonso Tozzi is a nice, friendly man, who instantly transmits his enthusiasm for his collection, a passion for which he has dedicated thirty years of his life, helped and encouraged by his wife.

The subject of his private collection of 27,000 razor blades with their illustrated wrappers, is not only curious and extraordinary, but also has an unimaginable historic, cultural and aesthetic value, which will surprise anyone, even those not interested in collecting, and even less so in razor blades.

With the discretion necessary on entering a private residence, collectors and those who are simply curious can make an appointment by telephone and be received in the Tozzi home to admire this exceptional collection. Sitting comfortably on a sofa in front of the albums in which thousands of paper wrappers are tidily classified in alphabetical order, one discovers that starting from the idea of a razor blade, the conversation can touch on an incredible variety of topics.

Prehistoric men began to shave with rudimentary obsidian blades, later replaced by flint and bronze blades. Razors continued to evolve, both in terms of the materials used to make them and in their shape, until in 1903 King Camp Gillette had the great idea of making a small steel blade, which was both robust and extremely thin, and could be fixed to a support and thrown away after use. In 1904, the Gillette Safety Razor Co. sold almost twelve and a half million blades.

From 1921, the year in which Gillette's exclusive patent ended, other blade manufacturers multiplied, staking everything, or almost everything, on the packaging, from the originality of the name to the graphic appearance of the product. They never imagined that forty years after this type of packaging disappeared, collectors the world over would reconstitute the tastes and daily life of the first sixty years of the 20th century in a fascinating way, thanks to these small coloured paper wrappers.

The colours, the styles, the themes are infinite; the slogans are funny and often disconcerting. You can thus discover razor blades inspired by sport, or by war and cannons. There are also blades inspired by 1930s cinema, by fascism, by animals, the city, the mountains, boats, aviation and so on.

ALPHABETICAL INDEX

ALPHABETICAL INDEX

THEMATIC INDEX

LIBRARIES

CURIOSITIES

CHILDREN

ESOTERICISM

OPTICAL ILLUSIONS

GARDENS – NATURE

THEMATIC INDEX

THEMATIC INDEX

Photography credits
All photos were taken by **Alessandra Zucconi** with the exception of:

Ginevra Lovatelli: Cannon ball of Viale della Trinità dei Monti fountain, Palazzo Zuccari, Andersen Museum, Squatriti, Goethe House, Criminology Museum, Vallicelliana Library, Angelica Library, Alexandrine Library, Staircase of Palazzo del Gallo di Roccagiovine, Vinegar-Makers' Arch, Monte Di Pietà chapel, Spada chapel, Boarded-Up window at Palazzo Mattei, Monumental complex of Santo Spirito in Sassia, Italian clock of the Palazzo del Commendatore, Foundlings' Wheel, Meridian at Saint Peter's, San Pietro in Montorio's cannon ball, Cloisters of the Nuovo Regina Margherita Hospital, Church bell at San Benedetto in Piscinula, Old pharmacy of Santa Maria della Scala, Orange tree of Santa Sabina Cloister, Sant'Alessio staircase, Catholic Cemetery, Table of Santa Barbara oratory, Museo Di Patalogia Del Libro, Magic Door, Blessing of the animals, Cannon Ball in the Aurelian Wall, House of Owls, Princess Isabelle's apartment, Pirandello's House, La Bottega del Soldatino, Magistri, Museo della Memoria Giocosa, Church of Tor Tre Teste, Museum of Period Coaches, Corviale (left page).

Jacopo Barbarigo: Traces of the Acqua Vergine, Trinité-des-Monts convent, Poussin's tomb, Cask of the Botticella Fountain, *The Dinner at Emmaüs*, Secret rooms of Saint Philip Neri, Blessing of expectant mothers, Mass in Aramaic, Stag of Sant'Eustachio church, Longinus Lance, Veronica's Veil, Tools for the holy door, Indulgences, Location of Saint Peter's crucifixion on Janiculum Hill, Villa Lante, Mosaic of Santa Maria in Trastevere, Argentarii Arch, Order of Malta, Triple enclosures, Santi Quattro Coronati basilica, Verbal abuse in Basilica san Clemente, Legend of Pope Joan, Grotesques, Statue of Stanislas Kostka, Meridians of Santa Maria degli Angeli, Flogging pillar of Santa Prassede.

Adriano Morabito: Mortuary Chamber of the Sextia Pyramid, Mithraic sanctuary of Circo Massimo, Other Mithraic sanctuaries, *Titulus Equitii* of the Basilica of San Martino ai Monti, Mussolini's bunkers at Villa Torlonia, Etruscan tomb of Villa Torlonia, Air-raid shelter in EUR district, Three columbaria of Vigna Codini, Cistern of Via Cristoforo Colombo, Hypogeum Cemetery of Santa Maria dell'Orazione e Morte church.

Marylène Malbert: Parrot Room, Catoptric sundial, the Wedding at Canaan *trompe-l'oeil*, Anamorphic frescoes of Trinità dei Monti convent.

Hélène Vuillermet: Abandoned infants bas-relief, Anatomy Theatre, American Academy, Headquarters of the Order of the Holy Sepulchre, History of Medicine Museum, Bernini's *Salvator Mundi*.

Brigante: Corviale (right page)
Jean-Pierre Cassely: Relic of Saint Marie-Madeleine
Prisca Curti: Vegetable garden of Santa Croce in Gerusalemme (right page)
Koen Ivens: Baker's Tomb
F. Lerteri: Hypogeum of Via Livenza, Excubitorium
Andrea Mazzini: Vegetable garden of Santa Croce in Gerusalemme (left page)
Science History Museum of Florence: "How does a meridian work?"
Corso Patrizi: Palazzo Patrizi
Beatrice Pediconi: Palazzo Sachetti (cover)
Carlo Pavia: Underground Tunnels of the Saint-John of Latran Hospital
Larco Placidi: Augustus sundial
E. Santucci: Jewish catacombs of Vigna Randanini
Palazzo Spada: Palazzo Spada
Enrico Sturani: Enrico Sturani
Unicredit Group: Hidden treasures of Roman banks
Aurora Pavilion: with the kind permission of Donna Maria Camilla Pallavicini
Alfonso Tozzi: Collection of razorblades

Acknowledgements: Dott. Aiello, Claudia Amadio, Luciano Antonini, Amici del Gonfalone Association, Florent Billioud, Philippe Bonfils, Maurizio Botta, Luisa Capaccioli, Jean-Pierre Cassely, Alessandra and Alessandro Corradini, Viviana Cortes, Laura del Drago, Fare fotografia, Fpmcom, Nunzia Fiorini, Tommaso Grassi, Giovanni Innocenti, Koen Ivens, Istituto di Studi Pirandelliani, Francesco Lovatelli, Beatrice Lovatelli, Marylène Malbert, Vincent Manniez, Andrea Mazzini, Flavio Misciattelli, Adriano Morabito, Dott. Paola Munafò, Dott. Muratore, Criminology Museum, Museum of Period Coaches, Hendrik Christian Andersen Museum, Nunzio, Simo Orma, Dott Petrollo Pagliarani, Donna Maria Camilla Pallavicini, Franco Palmieri, Corso Patrizi, Marco Placidi, Dominique Quarré, Maria Eleonora Ricci Parracciani Bergamini Massimo, Pierre Rosenberg, Neville Rowley, Pietro Ruffo, Palazzo Sacchetti, Giacinta Sanfelice, Maurizio Savino, Dott. Scialanga, Anna Maria Sciannimanico, Lorenzo Seno, Nicola Severino, Dott. Spalletti di Villa Spalletti Trivelli, Enrico Sturani, Mirtella Taloni, Marco Tirelli, Alfonso Tozzi, Caterina Valente, Delphine Valluet, Villa Médicis, Hélène Vuillermet.

Maps: **Michelin** – Map of Rome, authorization n°0501024. Copyright Michelin et Cie, 2004
Layout design: **Roland Deloi** – Layout: **Stéphanie Benoit** – English translation: **Caroline Lawrence and Vicki McNulty** – English editing: **Tom Clegg and Kimberly Bess**

In accordance with jurisprudence (Toulouse 14-01-1887), the publisher is not to be held responsible for any involuntary errors or omissions that may appear in the guide despite the care taken by the editorial staff.

Any reproduction of this book in any format is prohibited without the express agreement of the publisher.

© JONGLEZ 2012
Registration of copyright: June 2012 – Edition: 04
ISBN: 978-2-36195-042-2
Printed in France by Gibert-Clarey
37 170 CHAMBRAY-LES-TOURS